ROMNEY MARSH
SURVIVAL ON A FRONTIER

JILL EDDISON

One may not doubt that, somehow, good
Shall come of water and of mud;
And, sure, the reverent eye must see
A purpose in liquidity.

Rupert Brooke, *Heaven*

ROMNEY MARSH
SURVIVAL ON A FRONTIER

JILL EDDISON

Foreword by Barry Cunliffe

TEMPUS

First published 2000, reprinted 2000, 2004

Tempus Publishing Ltd
The Mill, Brimscombe Port
Stroud, Gloucestershire GL5 2QG
www.tempus-publishing.com

British Library Cataloguing in Publication Data.
A catalogue record for this book is available from the British Library.

ISBN 0 7524 1486 0

Typesetting and origination by Tempus Publishing.
Printed and bound in Great Britain.

Contents

The illustrations

The author is very grateful to the following institutions for permission to reproduce items in their collections: Cambridge University Committee for Aerial Photography (**33**, **38**, **47**), of which **33** and **47** are acknowledged as © Crown Copyright/MOD, reproduced with the permission of Her Majesty's Stationery Office; Public Record Office (**65**, **75**); the Warden and Fellows of All Souls College, Oxford (**colour plates 15, 25**); Institute of Archaeology, Oxford (**15a**, **15b**, **17**, **colour plate 8**); University College London Field Archaeology Unit (**13**, **colour plate 10**); Environment Agency (**colour plate 24**); Centre for Kentish Studies (**6**, **48**); Kent Archaeological Society (**26a**); and Maidstone Museum and Art Gallery (**23**, **24**), for which copyright remains with the Maidstone Borough Council. Figure **57** and **colour plate 22** are reproduced with the permission of the county archivist of East Sussex (copyright reserved).

Other photographs, maps and diagrams were supplied by the Cartographic Department in the University of Durham (**8**); Tony Balston (**colour plate 12**); Mrs Yvonne Bates (**colour plate 27**); David Eddison (**61**); C.R. Feilden, Esq (**colour plate 2**); Dr Mark Gardiner (**41-45**, **colour plates 7, 17, 18**); Professor John Hutchinson (**16**, **18**, **19**); Dr Ian Shennan (**colour plate 3**); Dr Chris Spencer (**colour plate 4**); and Dr Janet Stuart (**11**).

The rest of the photographs were taken by the author, and the black and white prints were made by Jon Rodger (**5**, **9**, **10**, **12**, **31**, **46**, **56**, **61**, **68**) and Mike Scutt (**11**, **54**, **63**, **64**, **70**, **71**, **74**, also **colour plate 4**). Mike photographed the All Souls maps (**colour plates 15, 25**), and the Symondson map (**57**). He also made copies of **63**, a 1930s newspaper cutting provided by the proprietor of the New Ship Inn, Winchelsea Beach and of **64**, a postcard loaned by Mr Kenneth Cook of Pett. James Eddison helped with scanning and photocopying, and with the production of keys to two diagrams. The help and interest of all these people is very gratefully acknowledged.

Particular thanks are due to Ian Agnew, who made fair copies of 28 of the author's hand-drawn maps.

Black and White Figures

The cover illustration shows Fairfield church set in a landscape of late twelfth- or early thirteenth-century ditches

Colour plates

1 A lesson in geological sampling
2 Extensive salt marshes at Stiffkey, north Norfolk
3 Fen carr
4 Peat, a mine of environmental information
5 The peat exposed on the foreshore near Pett
6 A Roman cremation assemblage
7 Scotney Court Quarry, a site of Roman salt-making
8 *Stutfall*, the Roman shore fort overlooking the Marsh
9 Baldwin's Sewer, a main drain cut in *c*.1150
10 Medieval landscape uncovered in a gravel quarry near Lydd
11 St Clement's church, Old Romney
12 St Nicholas' church, New Romney
13 The *Great Wall* where it defended Midley
14 The Rhee Wall at Old Romney
15 The Newlands estate belonging to All Souls College, mapped in 1589
16 The site of Broomhill church in 1983
17 The excavated north-west corner of Broomhill church
18 A burial at Broomhill
19 The progressive decay of Broomhill church recorded in a trench
20 New Gate, Winchelsea and part of the Town Ditch
21 Potman's Heath Cottage, Wittersham, perched on the *Knelle Dam*
22 The Craven Level, as mapped by Thomas Hill in 1688
23 Highknock Channel at Knock
24 Flooding at Bodiam in 1993
25 Camber and Broomhill mapped in *c*.1590
26 Camber Castle
27 Fairfield Church surrounded by flood water
28 Hazelden House, a cottage tilted as a result of peat wastage
29 Blackwall South Pumping Station, Wittersham Level
30 The Green Wall nearly breached
31 Defending the Dungeness power stations

Foreword

One of the many joys of excavating at the Roman Shore Fort of *Stutfall* in the 1970s was being invited by the owners of the site, Harry and Deirdre Margary, to their home at Lympne Castle built on the cliff edge above the Roman remains overlooking Romney Marsh. From the drawing room, added to the fifteenth-century castle by Lutyens, the panorama of the Marsh was spectacular. Its changing mood as the evening progressed, from the sharp clarity just before the light began to fade throwing into focus the white dots of individual sheep against the vivid green of the marshland pasture, through the greys and reds of evening, to the moonlit sheen of night, never failed to amaze. From high on the cliff at the edge of the Weald we were looking down on a secret, fragile world created by the constant interaction of the Channel currents and the Wealden rivers each struggling to deposit their loads of pebbles and sediments.

Most evenings after a day's excavating we drove down into this alien world to explore another corner. There can be few landscapes so redolent of the physical forces that created it and the human effort that has attempted to hold them in some kind of productive equilibrium. The man-made Dymchurch Wall, built to stop the sea from further eating away Romney Marsh proper, signals the victory of man over the sea, but the port of New Romney, now far from the sea, is a constant reminder that the combined power of rivers and coastal currents and subtle readjustments of sea level can be more than a match for puny human efforts. But it is Dungeness that makes the greatest impact. The huge expanse of shingle formed into monumental ridges by the ocean and the wind working together in a wild harmony is one of the great natural wonders of Europe. In the failing evening light the endless beach of loose shingle with its monstrous growth of sea cabbages and its line of lone fishermen facing the oncoming tide seem oblivious of the huge, dominating mass of the nuclear power station. The scene has the surreal quality of utter dislocation. Raw nature counterpoised with human arrogance. Perhaps this has always been the story of the Marsh.

Our excavations of 1976-8 and our attempts to present the results in the context of the evolution of the marshland landscape made us all too aware of what a neglected resource the Marsh was. But this was soon to change. In 1981 Jill Eddison gave a lecture to the Royal Geographical Society in the context of the rapid destruction of the historic landscape by modern farming. In doing so she set a new agenda and it was her energy which subsequently led to the creation of the Romney Marsh Research Group in 1983 to provide a multidisciplinary forum for the study of the Marsh. Since then the Group, later to become a Trust, has been a catalyst encouraging geomorphologists, archaeologists and historians to focus their efforts on this remarkable region. Four major conferences and three substantial monographs later, our knowledge has been revolutionized. Jill's intimate involvement with the research over the last 20 years, as a researcher in her own right and an enthuser of others, means that there is no one better to bring together the many strands into a cohesive story of a marshland landscape. For this, and the tireless efforts that lie behind it, we will be forever in her debt.

Professor Barry Cunliffe

Preface

Interest in the phenomenon of 'rising sea level' is increasing rapidly. As a result of the melting of ice sheets and glaciers, sea level has been rising in relation to the land since the last glaciation 18,000 years ago. Supposing it continues to do so, what will happen to the places that now lie at or below sea level? These include some of the world's major cities, starting with Venice followed not far behind by London, as well as very densely populated areas like most of Bangladesh, the Low Countries and the east coast of England.

Over and above the effects of rising sea level the coast of England is, and always has been, subject to continuous change. Most obviously, cliffs made of softer rocks collapse, carrying away or threatening houses and hotels. Less spectacular but more serious is the state of our lowland coastline. Only short stretches have been allowed to remain in their naturally evolving state. The rest is already protected by sea walls. Beaches are held in place by fields of groynes, and 'fed' with additional shingle from lorries or pipelines to replace that which the sea is busy removing and depositing elsewhere. Harbours need to be dredged to keep them clear of the silt deposited by the tides. Complex engineering structures are erected, often with unforeseen results that cause more problems than they solve. In short, man is attempting to maintain the *status quo*, and seeking short-term solutions to long-term problems, in a zone that is naturally altering at an alarmingly fast pace.

We cannot predict the future with any certainty, but a look at the past serves to illustrate some of the complexities of the interacting forces, the non-stop natural geological changes on the one hand, and man's attempts to intervene on the other. If we cannot predict the future, we can at least study the complex patterns of coastal changes in the past, and where better to do that than Romney Marsh? The historian Dugdale described it as the first large English marshland to be secured from the sea; its coastline has changed rapidly and radically with very serious impact on the inhabitants, and it is one of the best-researched of all the English marshlands.

This book stems from 15 years of multi-disciplinary work by the Romney Marsh Research Group, supported since 1987 by the Romney Marsh Research Trust. From the start Professor Barry Cunliffe has taken a keen interest and has provided support and encouragement in a variety of ways. And without the expertise of scholars across a wide range of disciplines, and their mutual collaboration, the story would not have begun to be unravelled. Quaternary geologists, whose attention is focused in this area on the last 10,000 years, were headed initially by Dr Michael Tooley and latterly by Dr Antony Long, Dr Andrew Plater and Dr Martyn Waller. As a medieval archaeologist Dr Mark Gardiner has drawn together the evidence of archaeology and historic documents, and led the work of archaeological teams from 1985 until 1999. Among historians who have contributed have been Dr Nicholas Brooks, Andrew Butcher and Dr Stephen Hipkin. Three monographs of papers have been published by the Trust, and a steady stream of papers is appearing in learned journals. The time has come to provide a synthesis of this wide-ranging academic work, and the object of this book is to do just that. It attempts to bring results of research into a more or less continuous narrative, and to set that in the very broad context of the environmental, economic, social and political forces that dominated occupation of the Marsh — and framed its landscape. It aims to make the results of very detailed research available to the general public, while at the same time providing a background which may be of use to researchers in the future.

A few words are needed to explain anomalies that will be encountered in the book. Ideally, the material should be arranged chronologically, and this is indeed the overall approach. However, complex events were taking place simultaneously in several widely-spaced and diverse areas, and therefore the story of each particular area has been carried forward to a logical break, before jumping sideways to see what was going on at the same time in another area. The valleys are dealt with in a separate chapter, because their story would over-complicate the Marsh chapters. Rye Bay is also taken on its own: it has evolved so recently that much more detail is known of coastal change there than anywhere else.

Certain expressions and situations have been simplified. It has been necessary to refer to some places a long time before they received names. For example, the southern half of the Marsh is generally described as Walland Marsh long before it received that name in the fifteenth century. And the shingle barrier is said to have grown out to Dymchurch several thousand years before that place existed. Modern spellings of place-names have been used. There was little consistency in the spelling of medieval scribes, and even less in the writings of the much more numerous, enthusiastic writers who followed them in the Tudor and Stuart periods. But why confuse the reader with *Bodyam, Bodihamme* or *Odyham*, when all the original writers were obviously referring to Bodiam? Winchelsea is a special case, for there were two Winchelseas. The first town and port was overrun and lost to the sea in the thirteenth century and replaced in 1280 by Edward I with the hilltop town we know today — safely out of reach of the sea. To avoid risk of confusion, the first town is referred to as *Old Winchelsea*, and its successor as New Winchelsea. Names of places that cannot now be identified on the ground, or names which have gone out of use are printed in italics — to save any enthusiastic readers from setting off in search of them. Some of the continental ports with which the medieval Marsh ports traded lay in *Flanders, Zeeland, Estland* and other states, all of which have changed their identities, their names and their boundaries since then. For simplicity, they are grouped together as the Low Countries.

River names have proved a very potent source of confusion. It was only after several centuries of human occupation that the local rivers were given the specific names we know today. That of the Rother was a sixteenth-century invention and the earliest known reference to the *Brede Ee* dates from 1382. In Saxon times, and perhaps more surprisingly in the medieval period, generic names such as *Limen, Ee, Rhee,* and *Channel* were used. Each of them simply meant a main watercourse. The local inhabitants knew very well which watercourse they were referring to as the *Limen*, but the nineteenth- and twentieth-century antiquarians and historians who tried to piece together early geography did not, and much confusion and controversy ensued. Recent research has ironed out some of that, and shows that *Limen* was used for at least two channels in the Saxon period. To complicate matters further, at least one *Limen* was not a river at all in the modern sense, but was simply a major creek where the tides flowed in and out, with little or no fresh water input!

Finally, a note about dates is needed. Geologists are able to measure the approximate age of organic deposits (mainly peat or wood, but occasionally shells) by their radiocarbon half-life. After any living organism dies, for example a tree falls or a salt-marsh plant dies, its carbon 14 isotope content is reduced at a known rate. By measuring the carbon 14 content of a sample it is therefore possible to work out the date that deposit was formed. Such dates are expressed in Years BP, ie Before Present, and the present is taken as AD 1950, because since that date the samples may have been contaminated by artificially-produced atomic fallout. On the other hand, archaeologists and historians use the familiar BC and AD timescale to provide a chronology of human affairs. In this book, in order to avoid the confusion which would inevitably arise from using two different scales, all the radiocarbon dates have been calibrated to take account of variations in solar energy in the past, converted to BC or AD as appropriate, and rounded off to the nearest hundred years.

The author owes thanks to an enormous number of people. Without the work of the specialists and their numerous assistants, the book could not have been written, and I am indebted to all of them for the stimulus of many discussions and enjoyable days in the field. We all owe thanks to the many farmers who have allowed us access to carry out fieldwork on their land. We are grateful to several organisations, especially the Sir James Colyer-Fergusson Charitable Trust, Robert Brett and Sons Limited and ARC Southern, and to numerous individual 'Friends' of RMRT for their support and enthusiasm. The appointment in 1989 of Dr John Williams as County Archaeological Officer brought new strength to the archaeology of Kent, with very positive results for the Marsh.

At the start of my own research I was encouraged by the late Professor J.A. Steers and also the late Professor Sir Harry Godwin, at Cambridge. More recently, I have been most grateful to two historians, Dr Joan Thirsk CBE, and Dr Mark Bailey for their kindness and patience with a non-historian attempting to get to grips with the complexities and implications of historical records. I have also been helped by the staff of the Canterbury Cathedral Archives (especially Dr Michael Stansfield), East Sussex Record Office (Christopher Whittick), the Centre for Kentish Studies (formerly the Kent Archives Office), the British Library, the Public Record Office, All Souls College, the Bodleian Library, the organisation which changed its name frequently, being known successively as the Southern Water Authority, Southern Water, or the Environment Agency, and by David Oliver now of the Internal Drainage Board. I derived much help and pleasure in the 1980s from discussions with Eleanor Vollans. Dorothy and Robert Beck frequently provide indispensable local knowledge, and for more than twenty years Clifford Bloomfield has generously shared his unparalleled knowledge of beach movements, historic maps and much else in the Rye area.

Dr Mark Gardiner and Dr Antony Long have kindly answered a constant barrage of questions connected with the book, and Gill Draper commented on three chapters of an early draft. The information on medieval Misleham stems from research carried out jointly with her. I am also grateful to Dr Martyn Waller, Luke Barber, Dr Stephen Hipkin, Dr Paul Cullen, David Martin, Anne Reeves, and to Richard Cross of the Canterbury Archaeological Trust for information. Dorothy Gray, having roamed the Marsh with me in all weathers for many years (nothing like a good storm for observing beach movements), has patiently struggled through drafts of every chapter. At a very late stage, Dr Joan Thirsk kindly read the manuscript. Her comments and suggestions have been invaluable and are greatly appreciated. Ultimately, however, the book inevitably reflects my own interests and opinions and I alone must take responsibility for what is written here.

Back at home, twenty years ago, a very youthful James Eddison decreed that 'we' needed a personal computer. How right he was. Since those early days of a *BBC*, he has repeatedly upgraded my equipment and helped me over many hurdles using it. Finally, my research would never have been accomplished, nor would this book have seen the light of day, without the encouragement and support of my husband, David.

1 Romney Marsh, a frontier

. . . the most civilized nations have by so much art and industry endeavoured
to make the best improvement of their Wastes, Commons and all sorts of
barren land. If the mere inclosure and tillage of that which naturally yielded
little profit doth justly deserve so great a commendation, how much more is
the skill and pains of those to be had in esteem, who have recovered many vast
proportions of land, totally overwhelmed with a deluge of waters?

William Dugdale, 1662
The History of Imbanking and Drayning of divers Fenns and Marshes

Romney Marsh is one of the three great coastal marshlands of southern England. In
common with the Fens of East Anglia and the Somerset Levels, and also the Humber
lowlands, the marshlands of north-west England and numerous other smaller areas round
our coasts, almost all of this large area lies below the level of high tides and has always been
under threat of flooding by the sea or fresh water; Dugdale's picturesque 'deluge of
waters'. But in one respect Romney Marsh is exceptional, and differs from the other major
marshlands. It alone developed and was originally occupied in the shelter behind wide
barriers of flint pebbles, known as shingle. These barriers provided not only essential
protection for the low-lying land, but also shelter for once-large anchorages on which
ports were based. However, rounded pebbles are moved all too easily by the waves and
therefore on a larger scale the barriers themselves moved. Thus a feature which had
provided essential protection in one century often became a liability in the next.

So where and what is Romney Marsh? It forms the south-east corner of England, and
in the widest sense includes 100 square miles (27,000ha) stretching 20 miles (32km) from
the cliffs near Fairlight in the south-west to those at Hythe in the north-east (**1**). On the
south and east it is bounded by the English Channel, with the great shingle promontory
of Dungeness jutting out towards France. On the west and north is an old cliff line cut
into the Wealden upland. Additional fingers of marshland extend up to 10 miles (16km)
westward along the valleys of three rivers, the Rother, Tillingham and Brede, with the
rivers providing important arteries into and out of the hinterland. This great expanse is
subdivided into several smaller areas, whose names generally date from the different times
at which they were reclaimed from the sea or when an autonomous authority was
established to manage their drainage. For many centuries the drainage of each of these
Levels was managed separately from the others. The largest, and those mentioned
frequently in this book, are Romney Marsh proper, lying to the north of the Rhee Wall (an

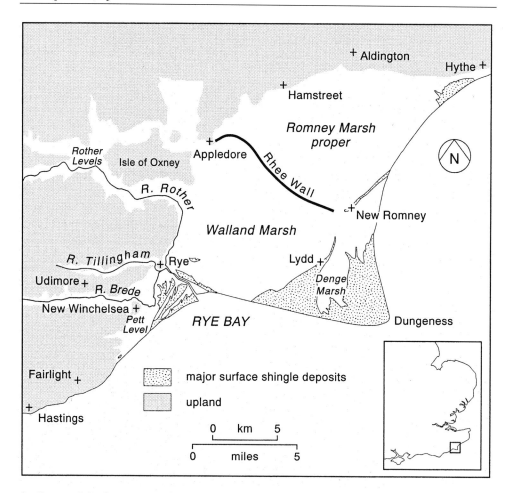

1 *Romney Marsh consists, in the widest sense, of one hundred square miles of coastal lowland beside the English Channel. The names of the principal drainage levels are written in italics. Note particularly the difference between Romney Marsh, the name applied in this book to the whole area, and Romney Marsh proper, the drainage level north of the Rhee Wall*

artificial medieval watercourse), and Walland Marsh to the south of that. Denge Marsh lies east and south-east of Lydd. Pett Level is to the south of Winchelsea. The Rother and Brede Levels include all the marshland in their respective river valleys. To avoid the confusion which would certainly arise if the same name were used to describe two different areas, throughout this book *Romney Marsh* (or simply *the Marsh*) is used to refer to the entire marshland, while *Romney Marsh proper* describes the smaller drainage Level.

This book describes the history of human occupation and survival on Romney Marsh, which has always been a frontier zone, on the border between dry land on the one hand and flooding by the sea or fresh water on the other. It is a story of interaction between the natural forces promoting continuous environmental change and human intervention usually trying to prevent that. It tells how men colonised potentially fertile land and by and large have retained it although the physical odds have been stacked against them. However, the delicate balance of the marshland frontier has depended on both the natural cycle of advance and retreat by the sea and on economic and social conditions. So it came about that land which was gained with admirable ingenuity and at great cost in one century was sometimes lost to the sea in the next. This is therefore a story of human adaptation to special circumstances that were always difficult and demanding, often fast-changing and sometimes overwhelming.

As soon as any part of the Marsh was occupied on a year-round basis an integrated system of protective banks, waterways and sluices was needed to get rid of river and rain water, and the present landscape holds invaluable evidence of how this evolved. Now, Romney Marsh is protected from the sea by a cordon of sea walls that fill the wide gaps between shingle barriers and sand dunes (**2**). Without the great Dymchurch Wall and others in front of Littlestone, Broomhill and Pett Level, high tides would very quickly convert parts, at least, of the Marsh back to salt marsh.

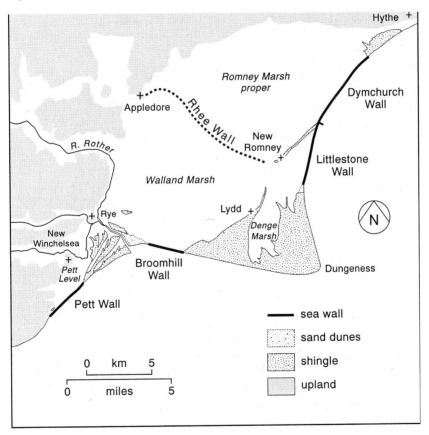

2   *The essential sea defences. Almost all of Romney Marsh lies below the level of the highest tides, so that high-level defences are essential to keep out the sea. Half of the cordon of defences consists of natural shingle banks and sand dunes. The other half consists of man-made sea walls*

Adding another dimension to the story, the Marsh also sits astride a cultural frontier. The coast of France is not much more than 20 miles (35km) away, visible on a clear day from some of the beaches of the Marsh. More important than that, it is possible to see the coasts of both England and France at the same time from a small boat out in the English Channel. So crossing the Channel was not tremendously intimidating, at least not when the weather was fine and the wind fair. Therefore the Channel should be seen as an historical highway as much as an obstacle to human movement (**3**). Indeed, there is abundant evidence of very close relationships with the Continent, closer perhaps at times than those with its English hinterland. Geographical circumstances favoured this. On one side was the Wealden upland, infertile and densely wooded, unattractive to settlement and a very wide barrier to communication (except for the relatively short river-highways). On the other hand, up to the end of the medieval period the Marsh was blessed with a sequence of fine natural harbours, where the larger ships could lie at anchor in channels and small boats could be tied up at the side, all sheltered and safe from the storms in the Channel, as illustrated in Prowez' marvellous sixteenth-century pictorial map (*see* **65**). The Marsh ports therefore naturally looked outward, across the Channel as well as along the English coast, and at various times the cross-Channel links were commercial, cultural, political and ecclesiastical.

The men of the ports were primarily fishermen, and secondarily had a well-earned reputation as pirates and wreckers. Sandwich, Dover, Hythe, Romney and Hastings emerged in mid-eleventh century as the Cinque Ports, the leaders among a large number of small channel ports. *Old Winchelsea* and Rye were added as equal partners some time before 1190. Besides their common but informal interest in fishing, and in the annual herring fair at Yarmouth, in the thirteenth century they were used by the Crown to provide defence for the coast and protection for cross-Channel traffic. But in the fourteenth century their political influence, which had been based on a monopoly of naval power and effective control of the Channel, declined rapidly. Throughout the medieval period (whenever cross-Channel politics permitted) there were also strong trading links with ports on the coast of continental Europe, mostly in northern France and the Low Countries. The merchants were frequently aliens, and it is likely that some formed small communities in the English ports. These were swelled on occasion by an influx of refugees. For instance, following the religious persecution and massacres in France in the 1560s, Rye became a haven of refuge for fleeing Protestants and had one of the largest foreign communities in Elizabethan England.

In the thirteenth and early fourteenth centuries, Winchelsea was the main port for importing wine from Bordeaux *en route* to London. Imports at New Romney in the fourteenth century included timber, building stone and Mediterranean foods such as garlic; exports included fish, corn, and dairy products from the Marsh. In mid-sixteenth century Rye flourished as an entrepot dealing with vast quantities of firewood from Wealden coppices and lesser amounts of oak timber, very bulky commodities which were floated down the Rother on lighters and then trans-shipped and forwarded across the Channel, notably to Calais. Until recently the evidence of cross-Channel trade came from documentary sources, but it is now being confirmed in field-walking exercises, and in archaeological excavations near Lydd, where significant quantities of medieval pottery

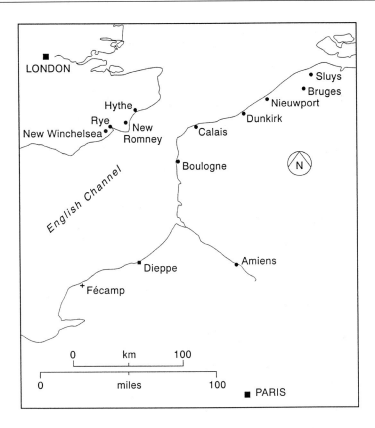

3   *The English Channel as an historical highway. In the medieval period the Marsh ports thrived*
on cross-channel trade, and this map shows some of the continental ports with which they traded.
The abbey of Fécamp in Normandy held the manor of Rameslie *which included* Old
Winchelsea *and* Rye *from c.1016-1247. Note that the coastline shown is that of today, and*
local details would have been very different in medieval times, on both sides of the Channel

made in France, the Low Countries or Germany have been found. That is a mere glimpse
of the international trade of the Marsh ports.

It is hardly surprising to find that men from the Low Countries, of necessity expert in
draining coastal marshes and the problems of silting harbours, were involved in similar
works over here. For instance, in 1410-13 Gerhard Mattheson from Holland supervised
the building of a new sluice for Romney. In 1440 John de Schiedamme requested that for
the next four years he might ship 1,000 pieces of tin from England free of customs dues,
because, as a result of his efforts, land previously of no value had been reclaimed near
Winchelsea and 'now much salt is made (there) to the great profit of the realm of
England'. In 1571 three men from Dunkirk and Nieuwport were involved in harbour
works at Rye. And in 1688 Mark le Pla from the Huguenot settlement of Thorney in the
Fens was commissioned by Lord Thanet to advise on intractable drainage problems in
Wittersham Level.

Politically and ecclesiastically there were also close links with the Continent. Relationships way back in the middle Saxon period are very uncertain, but it seems that at the end of the sixth and the beginning of the seventh century the King of Kent may have been subordinate to the King of *Neustria* (north-east France). In the medieval period French abbeys owned certain parts of the Marsh, the most notable of which was the vast Anglo-Saxon manor of *Rameslie* which included part of Hastings and, in due course when they developed, the towns and ports of *Old Winchelsea* and Rye. That manor was given to the Abbey of Fécamp on the Normandy coast by King Canute in *c.*1017, and remained in French hands until 1247. Then, because of the obvious strategic importance of the Channel ports at a time of hostilities, Henry III exchanged it for three inland manors in the West Country. Other French abbeys which had interests in the Marsh were Guînes, near Calais, and Pontigny, on the far side of Paris.

In war-time too, starting with the forays of third-century pirates, the Vikings in the ninth century, and Earl Godwin and his sons in 1052, the Marsh has been in the front line. Its flat coastline and gently-shelving beaches combined with the one-time tidal inlets and waterways have always been an open invitation to invaders, especially when compared to the steep cliffs of other parts of the coast between Hastings and Deal. Numerous defence works constructed at various times give us a gauge against which to measure the extent of coastal changes. For instance, the Roman shore fort of *Stutfall* now lies 1.5 miles (2.5km) inland on the hillside west of Hythe, although in the third century the sea must have come up to it.

From the great Renaissance topographers onwards the colourful history of Romney Marsh has attracted the interest and comments of antiquarians and historians. Leland in his *Itinerary* (1539) and Camden in *Britannia* (1586) were both aware that far-reaching changes had taken place in this coastline in the previous few centuries. Camden acknowledged his debt to William Lambarde, whose *Perambulation of Kent* had been published in 1576. This was the first county history to be written, and Lambarde can justly be called the father of local history. A pioneer, he believed firmly that the 'inwards of each place' were known best to those who lived there, and that it was they who should write their own histories. He was the first to draw attention to the specialised system of taxation which had evolved on Romney Marsh proper at an early date, laying a secure legal foundation for sea defence in an area very vulnerable to flooding. 'Romney Marsh', he wrote, 'is famous throughout the realm, as well for the fertility and quantity of the soil and Level, as also for the ancient and wholesome ordinances used for the preservation and maintenance of the banks and walls against the rage of the sea'. Those laws, written down in the face of potential disaster in the thirteenth century, had already become a 'pattern and example' later prescribed for the management of all similar marshlands in the country.

In the seventeenth century great interest centred on the possibilities of agricultural improvement. The East Anglian Fens were still vegetated open water or, at best, pasture which was flooded in the winter. To the progressively-minded this was a challenge, awaiting attempts to reclaim it. But any such proposals met with strong and violent opposition from the local inhabitants. As soon as political stability was established with the Restoration in 1660 Lord Gorges, the surveyor-general of the Great Level of the Fens insisted that William Dugdale, then Norroy King of Arms, should write a book in support

4 *William Dugdale, 1605-1686, was the first person to systematically accumulate a mass of data dealing with Romney Marsh. This shows him aged 50, in 1655. He copied a large number of historical documents into* The History of Imbanking and Drayning of divers Fenns and Marshes, *which was published in 1662 and is still a valuable source for historians*

of the 'adventurers' and their schemes for reclamation (**4**). The result was a magnificent volume, *The History of Inbanking and Drayning of divers Fenns and Marshes, extracted from Records, Manuscripts, and other Authentick Testimonies,* published in 1662. Having summarised reclamation of marshes abroad, he sought out and copied a great archive of historic documents dealing with English marshlands, arranged county by county and beginning with Romney Marsh. Whether this collection was relevant to Fenland proposals is doubtful, but it does provide the historian of Romney Marsh with very valuable basic material, not least because some of the documents he copied have since disappeared. On the other hand, some of Dugdale's personal conclusions, though delightful, have proved very misleading to later generations of researchers. He assumed that the whole of Romney Marsh proper had been enclosed at one time. Having found no records describing when or by whom it was won from the sea, he argued that it must be of great antiquity. 'The Britons', he wrote, 'were a people so rude and barbarous . . . not versed in any arts', and the Saxons 'so illiterate . . . that little invention can justly be ascribed to them.' He therefore concluded, noting their advanced civilisation, that the reclamation of Romney Marsh must have been the work of the Romans. It can now be proved that he was wrong.

A similar claim was made by James Elliott, the engineer in charge of rebuilding the Dymchurch Wall in the 1840s. The discovery of widespread evidence of Roman activity behind the wall inspired his interest in archaeology. He went on to assist Charles Roach Smith, the dentist who played a major part in rescuing the archaeology of London from Victorian redevelopers, in excavating *Stutfall*, the Roman fort which overlooked the Marsh. However, like those of Dugdale, his personal conclusions have proved misleading to later generations. He made the sweeping statement that 'Roman remains are found extensively over the whole area', from which he concluded that the Marsh was 'certainly under cultivation in the time of the Romans'. As an engineer he believed that sea defences were essential, so it was only a short step to decide that Romney Marsh proper had been reclaimed all at once by the erection of the Rhee Wall, by either the Romans or their precursors the Belgae. Unfortunately, however, it seems that he was guilty of exaggeration about his 'extensive Roman remains'. If, in fact, he had found any 'remains' other than those at Dymchurch and *Stutfall*, he has left no record of them and therefore his claim that the Rhee Wall was of Roman or earlier origin is very suspect.

In 1880 Canon Scott Robertson, an energetic and very thorough scholar, pointed out that the name *Rhee* means a watercourse, and showed that the landscape evidence confirmed this. Not until 1964, however, was scientific evidence produced to show that this complex and intriguing structure could not possibly be of Roman origin.

In the 1930s the Marsh became the focus of excellent work by scholars from a wide range of disciplines. W.V. Lewis, a Cambridge geographer, considered the evolution of Dungeness, the largest remnant of the shingle barrier that had once more or less enclosed the Marsh. R.A.L. Smith, a young historian also from Cambridge, studied the medieval documentary history of the estates of Christ Church Priory, Canterbury, noting particularly the techniques and economics of sea embankments and land drainage. Gordon Ward, a medical doctor and antiquarian from Sevenoaks, carried out brilliant detective work locating blocks of land mentioned in Anglo-Saxon land charters. Major Max Teichman Derville, long-term resident of Littlestone and mayor of New Romney, wrote a distinguished and detailed book on the administration of the *Level and Liberty of Romney Marsh* (proper). K.M.E. Murray, grand-daughter of James Murray of *Oxford English Dictionary* fame, wrote the *Constitutional History of the Cinque Ports*. Her introduction to the *Register of Daniel Rough*, the common clerk, provides a marvellous vignette of life in the port of New Romney in the fourteenth century. She worked closely with Teichman Derville. Ward, who also knew Teichman Derville, bridged the still-yawning gap between documentary history and the landscape with consummate success.

Otherwise, although the 1930s was the time when the Fenland Research Committee was pioneering an interdisciplinary approach elsewhere (proximity to Cambridge was no doubt an advantage), at that time research proceeded on Romney Marsh in several different disciplines but remarkably, each was still isolated from the others. The geographical work proceeded without an element of time, and that of the historians without a sense of place, with little or no reference to maps. Eventually, Ward and Lewis did meet at the Royal Geographical Society and agreed that it was essential for antiquarians (and implicitly historians) and geographers to pay close attention to each other's work. But that was in the dark days of March 1940, and World War II nipped that potentially fruitful phase of enquiry in the bud. The untimely deaths of both Lewis and Smith occurred soon after the War, and only Ward continued to publish in the early 1950s.

In the 1960s light began to dawn on an interdisciplinary approach from another, perhaps unexpected, direction. The Soil Survey of Great Britain published an extremely detailed study, *The Soils of Romney Marsh* (1968). For this, R.D. Green mapped the very intricate patterns of different soils across the Marsh on the basis of systematic, closely-spaced hand augering, mostly down to a depth of 42in (1.07m). He then incorporated landscape evidence and some historical records in an attempt to explain their relative dates and explain them in terms of the sequence of reclamation from the sea. His detailed map remains an essential reference for all future research.

From 1976 Professor Barry Cunliffe directed three seasons' archaeological excavation at *Stutfall*, the Roman fort below Lympne, and subsequently wrote a paper on *The Evolution of Romney Marsh,* significantly subtitled *A Preliminary Survey.* At much the same time Dr Nicolas Brooks published a paper on *Romney Marsh in the Early Middle Ages.* He used the early parish boundaries, together with the evidence of Anglo-Saxon land charters, Domesday Book (1086) and the local Domesday Monachorum of *c.*1100, to show that Romney Marsh proper had been occupied first and that some of the settlements there had later extended their holdings south-westwards down into Walland Marsh. Both those authors used the *Soil Survey* as a basis of their assessments, and both emphasised the immense value of the Marsh as a research resource. There was a great need for archaeologists, historians and geologists to collaborate if the secrets of the physical evolution and human history of the area were to be unravelled.

The time was ripe for a concerted multidisciplinary approach. A lecture given by the author to the Royal Geographical Society in 1981, followed by a letter from her protesting about the widespread destruction by ploughing of hundreds of hectares of historic landscape with its unique visual record of progressive reclamation from salt marsh, provided the catalyst. In 1983 Professor Cunliffe convened the first meeting of the Romney Marsh Research Group. This was the beginning of intensive study of the evolution and history of the Marsh, with regular collaboration between the geologists, archaeologists and historians, and in 1987 the Romney Marsh Research Trust was established to support the work financially.

All research involves collection of a large amount of information, or data, followed by skilled analysis attempting to make sense out of the patterns that emerge. On the Marsh there is a wide variety of sources of information, to which a wide variety of research methods can be applied. The obvious starting point is the historic landscape. At a quick

5   *Surviving historic marsh landscape, Broomhill in 1999. It is strikingly flat, and every micro feature has a story to tell. This pasture was formerly a high, vegetated salt marsh, and is still dissected by very sinuous, former creeks. This area, near the south coast of Walland Marsh, was gained and lost several times, before being finally enclosed by walls in c.1585. The horizon is formed by the present-day Broomhill sea wall, with the coastguard cottages on the left. The scar in the foreground was caused by the land-rover used by the farmer for shepherding*

glance, the Marsh is a flat, windswept land, criss-crossed by sewers (the historic name for the main drains which take the surface water away to the sea), innumerable minor ditches and a variety of raised banks. Every ditch and bank has a story to tell, and every change in land-level, however slight, is significant. Different patterns of the fields (large or small, rectangular or irregular), of the sewers and walls reflect not only different economic and social conditions of the time that land was gained from the salt or freshwater marsh, but also variations in environmental conditions such as changes in the coastline, the water table, and the river and sewer courses. It is, or was, a very special landscape. On the eve of World War II the Marsh still consisted almost entirely of 'traditional' sheep pasture, most of which dated from medieval times (**5**). But since then, in the latest agricultural revolution, most of the pasture has been ploughed up and levelled. Sub-surface tile drains have been installed, and the earth which formed the old sea banks has been used to fill in redundant ditches and fleets (incidentally, wonderful havens for wildlife). Now 90% of the Marsh is arable. To find remaining nuggets of historic landscape researchers and visitors should, for example, walk the lanes north of Brookland, take to the footpaths in East Guldeford and Broomhill or drive slowly along Lower Wall, the road leading from Newchurch towards West Hythe.

    To reconstruct the details of a landscape now largely lost, the archaeologists turn to aerial photographs and early maps. They also survey surviving earthworks and the few standing buildings that constitute the architectural heritage. Archaeological excavations provide a large amount of very detailed information on the nature of human occupation and activities, but are usually concerned with areas that are very small indeed compared to the vast expanse of the Marsh. Other methods have the advantages of covering wider areas than most excavations, of being carried out on the surface without disturbing the ground and interrupting farming activities, and are much less expensive. These include field walking, which is the systematic collection on a grid of artefacts (usually pottery and metal objects) from ploughed fields. Geophysical methods can be used to identify changes in density below the surface, and hence a resistivity survey was used to great effect at Broomhill church (*see* **41**). Metal-detectors are a useful tool, although a note of caution is needed. It is essential that the exact location and depth of the finds are recorded, details which are often lost in the hands of amateur enthusiasts.

The survival of historic documents is a lottery. Innumerable records were kept only to be discarded, lost, burnt by accident or wilfully destroyed as expressions of hate for an existing or previous regime; for instance in the Peasants' Revolt in 1381 or the Commonwealth of 1649-60. It is therefore fortunate that in the medieval period a very large part of the Marsh was owned by institutions whose documents have a relatively high survival rate, namely several monasteries, the Archbishop of Canterbury and two Oxford colleges. Their surviving archives include an enormous number of charters and estate records dealing with many aspects of Marsh history, including land drainage and sea defence. From the thirteenth century onwards there are also royal statutes and the records of central government. The special nature of the Marsh, where land drainage and sea defence were a priority, means that the drainage authorities kept extraordinarily detailed records. For Romney Marsh proper, Walland and Denge Marshes, and for part of the Rother Levels, these provide a very full record of the battle against the waters from the seventeenth century onwards, while scattered material provides glimpses into the previous century (**6**). There are enough records of the Dymchurch Wall alone to keep a small team of workers happily employed for several years.

A large number of maps survive, mainly dating from 1589 onwards, while one or two are even earlier. They are generally extremely accurate, are especially helpful in bridging the gap between the written documents and the landscape and, since many are beautifully coloured works of art, are very attractive tools to work with. Most of them were drawn to explain the special problems faced in the area. A number illustrated the critical silting of Rye harbour, which happened to coincide with great advances in the science of cartography. Others were drawn in connection with the collection of the scots to pay for sea defence and land drainage, especially on Romney Marsh proper and in the Rother Levels.

Because the Marsh has been built up, layer upon layer over thousands of years, an almost complete record of environmental history and change is contained in the sediments lying beneath it. In order to identify and sample these deposits, the geologists use tools known as augers (**colour plate 1**). Borings are put down along a line described as a transect, and a continuous narrow core is retrieved at each. At each site details of the sediments, and their exact level in relation to Ordnance Datum, are very carefully recorded (**7**). Then a wider auger may be put down to collect samples to be sent back to the laboratory to be analysed in even greater detail. The nature of the sediments, and the

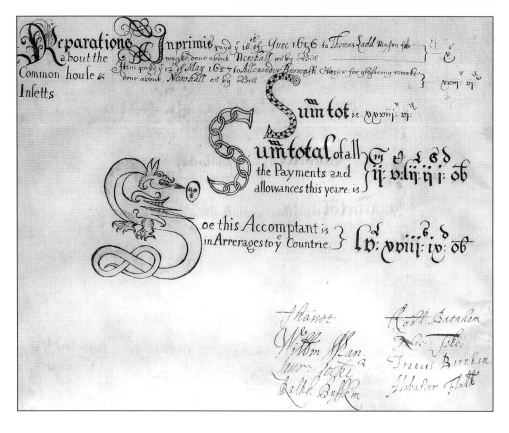

6   *The cost of maintaining the Dymchurch Wall in 1656/7. This is the last page of the Expenditor's Account for the financial year which ran from 29 May 1656 to 21 May 1657. The expenditor for that year, Zouche Brockman gent., illustrated it with a flourish. All the sums are in Roman numerals. At the top are the entries under the very last heading, repairs to New Hall at Dymchurch, which came to a total of 28s 6d. Below that is the total amount paid in the year, which amounted to £2,552 2s 1½d. The arrearages of £55 18s 9½d consisted of money which was due to the expenditor but had not yet been paid when the account was made up.*

    The Lords of all the 23 Marsh manors were nominally responsible with the Bailiff and the Jurats for the upkeep of the Dymchurch Wall, but only a minority of them took an active part. This account is signed by the eight who attended the annual meeting (general lathe) on 21 May 1657, headed by Lord Thanet. From CKS S/Rm FAe 28

plants and organisms contained in them, are examined under a microscope and eventually a few representative samples may be sent off to specialist laboratories for radiocarbon dating (*see* note on page 15).

    Each line of research is pursued by specialists with different specific skills. They then need to come together to discuss their results and theories. This book presents the results of such a multidisciplinary approach.

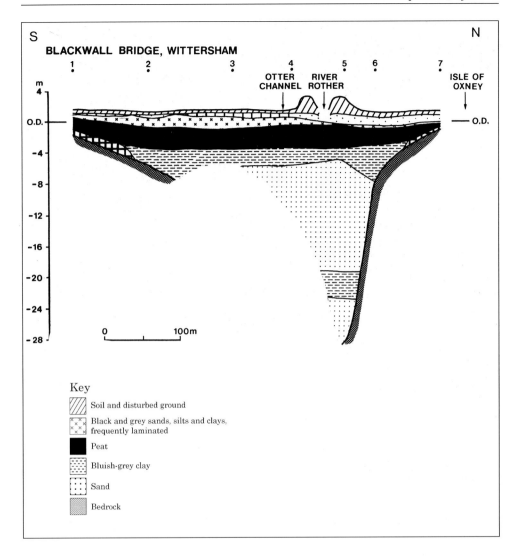

7 *What lies beneath the surface. A geological section across the Rother valley at Blackwall, south of the Isle of Oxney, drawn by Dr Martyn Waller on the basis of information from the seven bore-holes numbered across the top. Note the deep channel cut by the river into the solid Wealden rocks in the Ice Age, and various soft sediments which filled the valley, keeping pace with rising sea level (see 8). The thick layer of peat has proved very troublesome for both river management and land drainage*

2 The legacy of the Ice Age

The origins of the Marsh and its setting go back to the Ice Age, when the surrounding arc of Wealden hills and valleys acquired their present outline, and a vast quantity of flint nodules was released from the chalk of southern England. Two and a half million years ago the earth began to cool and the polar ice sheets began to expand outwards, combining with mountain glaciers on their way. For much of the time since then our climate has been predominantly cold, and sediment cores taken recently from deep beneath the oceans have shown that relatively long-lasting, intensely cold periods have alternated with shorter, much warmer intervals when elephants and other tropical beasts roamed in the Thames valley. Ice sheets therefore advanced and retreated several times across England. At their greatest extent they came as far south as the northern outskirts of London. They never reached Romney Marsh.

However, although southern England was never glaciated there were long periods when it was in the grip of very severe winters. During those winters the land there rested, lying undisturbed beneath a blanket of snow. But as soon as the temperature rose in spring, the melt water became an extremely potent force. With warm days but very cold nights, the action of freezing and thawing broke up the chalk of the Downs between Sussex and Dorset to the south-west of our area, releasing the flint nodules embedded in it. The upper layers slid off their frozen base of permafrost and avalanched or slumped down the steep hillsides, in a consistency similar to lumpy porridge. Most of the soft and soluble chalk was broken down and carried off in solution. But the much harder, more resistant and insoluble flint was carried down the valleys by seasonal flood waters and eventually reached the floor of the English Channel.

During the cold periods, sea level was lowered by as much as 400ft (120m) because so much of the earth's water was locked up in the ice sheets away to the north. The sea therefore retreated down the Channel to the vicinity of Cornwall. This had a knock-on effect on the rivers, all of which cut deeply down into the bottom of their valleys, working to a lowered base level and helped by powerful seasonal surges of melting snow. For example, at Blackwall Bridge in Wittersham Level, south of the Isle of Oxney, the Ice Age Rother cut down some 100 ft (30m) into bedrock below the present bottom of the valley (see **7**). The Brede and the Tillingham have similarly deep-cut valleys. Since then, the valley bottoms have been filled with a variety of soft sediments, more or less keeping pace with the rise in sea level. As a result, as we see them today the valleys have steep sides and flat bottoms, and are also surprisingly wide considering the small size of the rivers.

The Wealden upland which forms the backdrop to the Marsh, and through which the valleys have been cut, is formed of a variety of Cretaceous rocks some 120 million years old. The arc of hills changes as we follow the sweep round, according to the types of rock which form it (*see* **1**). Vertical cliffs near Fairlight and Rye are cut in hard sandstones of the Hastings Beds (*see* **64**). They give way to much gentler slopes of Weald Clay near Appledore and Hamstreet. Further east, between Aldington and Hythe, the clay is capped by a limestone known as Kentish Ragstone, a combination which produces hummocky, landslipped hillsides.

In contrast to those relatively hard rocks, the sediments of the Marsh and valleys have accumulated, layer upon layer, in the last 10,000 years — and the upper layers have only been laid down within the last 2,000 years. Indeed, silt is still being deposited in the Rother estuary, and new shingle ridges are being built out on the east coast of Dungeness. The very abrupt contrast between the slopes of the upland and the strikingly flat surface of the Marsh reflects that difference in age. Thus, if he stood with one foot on the Marsh and the other on the edge of the upland, a man could bridge a vast interval in geological time.

Eighteen thousand years ago, when the most recent ice sheets and glaciers began to melt, the Marsh area must have been a very desolate place. As far as we know from the very limited evidence available from a surface now buried 100ft (30m) down, it was rough, irregular, and covered with a veneer of frost-shattered rock fragments, with minimal sub-arctic vegetation. What is now the floor of the English Channel was littered with a vast array of flints. This legacy of the Ice Age was to have a vital significance for Romney Marsh.

The water that had been locked up in the ice sheets gradually returned to the sea, and from that time forward it was the forces of the sea that formed and shaped the Marsh. Initially sea level rose very rapidly, crossed the continental shelf and came back up the English Channel. Until about 6,000 years ago it continued to rise quickly, and then the rate slowed down, only to start rising more quickly again about the beginning of the first millennium AD (**8**) (*see* the note on dating methods on page 15). At present the sea defence authorities base their calculations for keeping the sea out of the Marsh on a rise of 0.24in (6mm) per year (1ft or 30cm in 50 years).

When the sea returned, high tides and high-energy waves of the English Channel came up to the edge of the upland, and the whole Marsh area became a great sandy bay. Seaside holiday-makers, had there been any, would only have needed to visit Appledore or Hamstreet rather than travel out across the Marsh to Dymchurch or to Camber Sands near Rye. At that time there would have been no reason to predict that the Marsh as we know it would ever exist.

But about 6,000 years ago onwards three different geological stories unfolded more or less simultaneously. Firstly the sea began to build out a massive shingle beach in a north-easterly direction across the sandy bay, which was the first crucial step in the formation of the Marsh. Without this barrier (described for obvious reasons as a *barrier beach*) the Marsh as we know it would certainly not have existed, and a very dramatic human history would never have happened.

This barrier which separated the Romney Marsh area from the open sea is therefore of fundamental importance to our story. Its evolution followed a three-stage pattern typical of innumerable offshore barriers around the world, and it is not unlike that of the life of a human being. The first, youthful, stage was one of rapid enthusiastic development: it

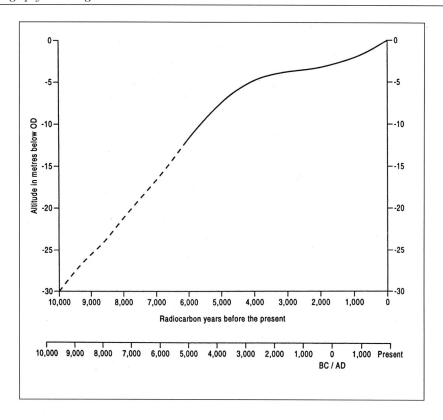

8   *A graph showing the rise in sea level in the last 10,000 years in the Romney Marsh area, based on radiocarbon dates obtained from numerous samples of the peat which underlies the Marsh, and other carbonaceous materials. The upper time scale along the bottom of the graph shows the radiocarbon dates in years BP (Before the Present, which is taken as 1950), based on work by Dr Andrew Plater and others. In the lower time scale the dates have been calibrated and converted to BC/AD, no doubt more familiar to most readers.*
Note also this graph is very different to one published in the 1930s, which had sea level bouncing up and down like a yo-yo and was not based on reliable geological or archaeological data

grew quickly out across the bay and soon extended as far as the later site of Dymchurch (*see* **14** for its general position). The second stage was one of maturity and consolidation in which, as the waves continued to bring massive quantities of shingle along the outside of the beach from the south-west, the barrier became broader and the great promontory of Dungeness began to build out. The third stage was that of old age: the shingle of Dungeness was redistributed so that the 'ness' became more prominent. But elsewhere, with little or no new shingle arriving from the south-west, the barrier broke up into separate segments. Permanent breaches occurred near New Romney and Rye, further breaches threatened, and the gaps in the barrier had to be plugged by sea walls. As this book describes, the breaches were a very mixed blessing as far as the human inhabitants were concerned. We are now living with the third stage of its life, with the barrier broken

9 *Storm waves reaching the coast at Broomhill at an angle, 'travelling' along the beach and throwing shingle eastwards, towards the camera, in the process known as* longshore drift. *The groynes were put there to impede this movement of shingle, but as their landward end has been broken away by the action of the sea, they are now not much use. The Fairlight hills can be seen in the background, across Rye Bay*

asunder — the result of this continuous change, and about half the present coast has to be guarded by sea walls (*see* **2**).

How has this happened? The sea is in a constant state of movement, with a non-stop procession of waves reaching the coast. These throw the shingle forward, up the beach, which explains why in many places the top of the beach is stony while the lower parts are sandy or muddy. Also, when the waves break on the coast at an angle they 'travel' along the shore and throw the pebbles forward diagonally (**9**). As the dominant winds here come from the south-west, the waves also come from that direction and 'travel' from west to east along the south coast of England, bringing shingle with them. On a calm day this process, known as longshore drift, is almost imperceptible. On the other hand in the big storms every wave will move a lorry-load of beach, the noise of grinding pebbles is deafening and an observer will find it impossible to keep pace with the shingle as the waves carry it round the point of Dungeness. Longshore drift, as we shall see, caused many of the greatest difficulties suffered by the local inhabitants throughout history, and the greatest movement has taken place in the spasmodic and unpredictable great storms. The results have been widespread flooding, erosion of inhabited sites, loss of livestock and, occasionally, of human life.

It was by means of longshore drift that, as sea level rose after the ice sheets melted, the waves picked up increasing quantities of shingle from the floor of the Channel and brought it up towards the present coast, moving it eastwards all the time. The Romney Marsh coastline was to be its final destination, and an exceptionally large volume has ended up in the 'sink' of Dungeness, making that the most important accumulation of flint shingle in north-west Europe.

With a continuing supply arriving from the south-west, the waves banked up one shingle ridge after another, each new one outside the last. Eventually there were well over 600 ridges in the Dungeness mass, extending 7 miles (11km) from west to east (including early ridges, now buried), 4 miles (6.5km) from south to north, and increasing to a depth of some 22ft (6.5m) towards the ness. Since every ridge was at one time the front-line beach, by plotting the ridges using aerial photographs it is possible to make maps of early coastlines (**10**). And because sea level has been rising all the time Dungeness has been forming, the tops of some of the earliest ridges are some 16ft (5m) below those of the present day beach. For the last 4,000 years the waves have acted as a conveyor belt, moving shingle along the south coast of the Dungeness mass and building up new ridges on the east coast. This means that shingle is being constantly lost from the south coast, so that is retreating while the east coast is growing outwards. The problems this causes for the Dungeness nuclear power stations which were built close to the south shore in the 1960s and '70s are discussed in chapter 10.

The Dungeness promontory contains a wealth of information, an almost complete record of coastal changes and past storms. On the other hand, the parts of the original

10 *A small part of the Dungeness shingle mass, seen from the top of the old lighthouse, with the station on the Romney, Hythe and Dymchurch Light Railway in the foreground. The shingle ridges shown here have accumulated since 1800. Each ridge was built outside the last when a fresh supply of shingle arrived by longshore drift, probably in a storm. The oldest are at centre left, and the present coastline is beyond the line of bungalows in the distance*

11 A typically sinuous salt-marsh channel, alternatively known as a creek, at Morston, north Norfolk. It is nearly dry at low tide, with an equally sinuous stream of water draining away in the bottom. It is filled by every high tide, and the extensive vegetated salt marsh in the background is covered by spring tides and in storms. The boats are tied up and left to sink into the mud of the creek at low tide, which must have been the practice in Romney Marsh channels in past centuries

shingle barrier which lay across Rye Bay, Romney Bay and protected the Dymchurch coast have all gone, all the pebbles having been moved on and recycled (geologists describe them as being *reworked*). So, as we shall see in the chapter on Rye Bay, attempts to reconstruct the evolution of those parts of the coast can only be based on indirect information, including that from archaeological and historical sources.

Secondly, when the barrier developed it created a sheltered lagoon behind it, and set in train a sequence of environmental changes there. The tides flowing in round the northern tip of the barrier carried a load of fine-grained sediments, clay, silt and a minor quantity of sand suspended in the water. Towards high tide the flow of water slowed up, and its load sank to the bottom, remaining behind when the tide seeped quietly away again. The lagoon became mudflats, and as more sediment accumulated this became high enough to be colonised by a succession of fleshy plants specially adapted to living in a salt-water environment. These plants trapped more sediment, and the tidal flow became restricted to sinuous channels, winding their way between clumps of vegetation (**colour plate 2**). A vegetated salt-marsh platform was established above the level of all but the highest tides, dissected by characteristically winding channels (**11**). The salt marsh continued to grow

35

upwards and outwards faster than sea level rose, so that the sea retreated until the lagoon was restricted to only the north-east and centre of Romney Marsh proper. Then, around 1000BC, the pendulum swung and the sea began to re-advance slowly, since sea level was then rising faster than the marsh was building up.

Thirdly, a different picture emerges from the valleys. Initially the sea flowed some distance up the valleys, but soon rising sea level blocked the outflow of river water and the valleys became waterlogged, and freshwater swamps known as fen carr developed, with thick vegetation dominated by alder trees (**colour plate 3**). These conditions were self-perpetuating, with new trees and plants growing on top of the decayed remains of previous generations, and so continued for some 3,000 years. Similar fen carr developed along the landward fringe and spread quickly outwards across the Marsh while, in contrast, the centre of Walland Marsh near Little Cheyne Court became an acidic raised bog with sphagnum, heather and birch.

Remarkably, the vegetation of both salt marsh and fen carr has survived, as peat. Usually dead vegetation rots away because of the action of the oxygen in the air and of numerous small organisms. But on the Marsh it was below the water-table and then was sealed in by layers of impervious sediments brought in by the sea, and so it stayed out of reach of the oxygen (**colour plate 4**). However, when the water-table is lowered by over-efficient land drainage and the peat is exposed to the air, it wastes away, lowering the land-surface and causing further problems for the drainage authorities.

Victorian antiquarians thought this interesting-looking black deposit of tree trunks lying in a bed of leaves must have been washed down from the Weald by some primeval flood! However, since the roots of trees can now be seen *in situ*, where they grew, it is no longer necessary to invoke that fantastic echo of Noah. Peat can be seen low down in some sewers, but it is best seen below mid-tide level on the foreshore outside the Pett sea wall, especially after storms have swept away the beach sand (**colour plate 5**). Containing leaves, roots, twigs, wood and, most important of all, innumerable grains of pollen, it provides the scientist with a vast encyclopaedia of information about past environments, and the age of samples can be measured by the radiocarbon method described on page 15. The results can be used to date not only the peat but the deposits beneath it. Thus, while the barrier was building outwards and upwards, finer-grained sediments were building up in the lagoon behind the barrier and burying some of the early, low-lying shingle ridges. At Tishy's Sewer north-east of Broomhill (named after the observant person who noticed an interesting sequence exposed after a sewer had been cleaned out), peat preserved on top of shingle between two low-level ridges was found to have formed in *c*.1600BC. This proved that the first shingle was in place there sometime before that date.

Progressive accumulation of one layer of sediment after another is very helpful to geologists because it provides a nearly complete record of early environments, but it is also a fundamental problem for archaeologists. How can evidence of early activity and/or occupation be found when it is hidden beneath a blanket of later sediments perhaps one or two metres deep? Over an area of 100 square miles (27,000ha), it is like looking for the proverbial needle in a haystack. Until the 1980s, whereas scatters of Mesolithic (in general terms 8300 to 4000 BC) and Neolithic (4000 to 2000 BC) flints had been found on the upland, nothing of prehistoric significance had been found on the Marsh itself (though as

12 *Bronze Age and Iron Age finds distributed along the back of the shingle near Lydd. This evidence of pre-historic activity has come to light during archaeological investigations in advance of gravel quarrying. Without the quarries, it would have remained buried and undiscovered beneath a blanket of later sediments*

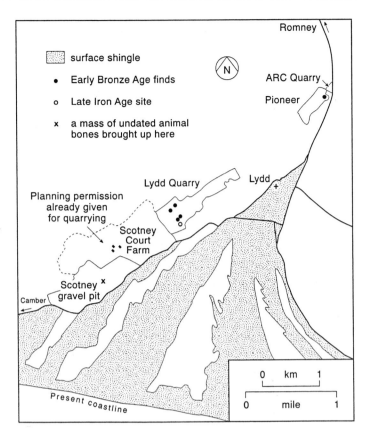

that flint must have come from the beach, it does show that there was already a local trade between coast and hills at that early date). Finds on the Marsh only amounted to a very few arrowheads lying on the surface, which at that high level seemed to have been collectors' items dropped recently and had to be ignored as serious evidence, and a broken bronze blade found on the coast between Pett and Fairlight in 1937.

There was therefore considerable excitement when it became known that five Early Bronze Age axe heads had come up in the Pioneer gravel quarry a mile (1.5km) north of Lydd in 1985 (**12**). These only came to light because of a series of lucky accidents, since they must have been brought up out of the quarry by a drag line machine and shovelled around the plant site before they were spotted by a very observant worker monitoring a conveyor belt. Even then, they were taken to a local pub on the night they were found, and were separated and passed through several different hands before the first of them was submitted to the British Museum two months later. Such are the adventures of random finds. The axes dated from *c*.1800 BC, and in archaeological terms were described as a hoard. They had probably been purposely buried, possibly in a hurry. Alternatively, they may have been dumped by accident when a ship was wrecked close to the shore. Either way, the find was of tremendous importance. Much has been written about the export of such axes, which probably originated in Ireland, to northern Europe. And here was evidence that the local shingle barrier, the embryo Dungeness, was being used as a staging post on the way to Europe. Four thousand years ago Romney Marsh was already on a significant sea-trading route.

This was not only the first indication of a prehistoric presence on the Marsh, it was also of great importance as it provided a general date by which this part of the barrier was undoubtedly in place. Although the exact depth and original stratigraphical position of the axes is not known, they must have been lying either on or buried in the shingle. This date provided by archaeological means was remarkably similar to that which had previously been deduced for shingle at a similar altitude and similarly near the back of the barrier at Tishy's Sewer, Broomhill, from radiocarbon dating of peat above it. While this proved that there were indeed buried prehistoric horizons, we were unfortunately no further forward in knowing where to look for such material.

Then, a further opportunity to investigate buried horizons opened up in 1990, when planning permission was given for very extensive gravel extraction, expected to take place progressively over 20-30 years, this time to the south-west of Lydd (*see* **12**). The area concerned followed the trend of shingle ridges along the back of the barrier for 2.5 miles (4km) from south-west to north-east. The operation was to involve near-total removal of not only a vast area of shingle and all the finer-grained sediments that lay on top of it (known to the quarrymen as the overburden), but also all the geological and archaeological evidence it might contain. The geological deposits held several very important keys to understanding the early development of the shingle barrier and the evolution of the marsh behind it, and as the site lay within the Dungeness Site of Special Scientific Interest, a complete geological study of the area was undertaken before quarrying began, funded by the developer, Robert Brett & Sons Ltd.

Progressive exposure of such a large area where sedimentation had built up roughly keeping pace with rising sea level also presented a magnificent, probably unequalled opportunity for investigation of buried landscapes. The Bronze Age axes found to the north of Lydd had been in a similar position on the barrier, so it seemed likely that the new quarry might well produce further evidence of prehistoric occupation. There might be archaeological evidence going back several thousand years which otherwise would have been obscured forever beneath later deposits of sand, silt or clay.

One of the conditions attached to the planning permission was that the developer should make financial provision for archaeological investigation before the shingle was extracted. The problem was how to deal with such a vast area, of potentially great but still unknown interest, there being no technological means of exploring the potential before the topsoil was stripped off. An archaeological strategy was decided by Dr John Williams, the Archaeological Officer for Kent County Council, and Dr Mark Gardiner, then Deputy Director of South East Archaeological Services. All the archaeological features revealed when the topsoil had been stripped off were to be mapped and recorded, in one small area after another. This was to be followed by selective excavation of any particularly interesting features.

At a very early stage, during the initial investigation at the future plant site in 1991, a barbed-and-tanged arrowhead of Early Bronze Age date (the second millennium BC) was found lying on top of a shingle ridge, together with four pieces of worked flint (**13**). The promise of this find was borne out very soon afterwards, when a concentration of Roman

13 *An Early Bronze Age flint arrowhead from Lydd Quarry, evidence of hunting in that area in the second millennium BC. It was found by archaeologists in 1991, when the ploughsoil was stripped off the future plant site at the Brett Gravel quarry. It was originally attached to a wooden shaft*

artefacts (described in the next chapter) was found nearby. This one arrowhead did not provide a great deal of information about prehistoric exploitation of the marshland, but it did suggest hunting was taking place, a suggestion which tied in with a very large concentration of bones, including some of red deer, which had been dredged up with the overburden at Scotney Court quarry, nearly a mile (1.5km) further south-west some years previously (*see* **12**).

Quarrying went ahead and in 1996 the archaeological watching brief, undertaken every time a new area of topsoil was removed, was rewarded. Several clusters of Early Bronze Age pottery dating from the second millennium BC were found lying along 140 yards of the crest of a shingle ridge, possibly marking the route of a prehistoric trackway. Over 200 pieces of worked flint including cores and scrapers of Bronze Age type and a large quantity of burnt flint were also found. Although the flints could not be dated specifically, they were found lying beneath a Roman level, and were therefore older than that. In the next two years two small hearths and a pit were found associated with worked flint and large quantities of fire-cracked flint pebbles. And in 1998 a number of similar small hearths were found in a small quarry which was opened up by ARC for a few months 1.25 miles (2km) north of Lydd church.

The hoard of Early Bronze Age axes showed that the shingle barrier, the uttermost point of land, was on the map of trade routes to the Continent, and probably also had connections with Ireland. Otherwise activities appear to have been of a more local nature. The flint was being used as raw material for on-site manufacture of tools and weapons, and the arrowhead shows that some hunting, at least, was taking place locally. The hearths may have been the basis of short-stay camps used by people who were either flint-working or hunting, or both, but whether there were very small groups of men who came out on to the shingle occasionally, or a larger group who visited less frequently, is impossible to say. So far, the only dateable material had come from the Early Bronze Age.

Until 1998 there had been a marked lack of evidence of any kind of built structure. Then, an arrangement of 17 upright timbers was found, sunk 2ft (60cm) into a bed of silty clay, close to a large silt-filled channel approximately 80ft (25m) wide and up to 23ft (7m) deep. The timbers may have supported a deck 7ft (2m) wide, which could have served as a causeway across the channel, or alternatively may have provided access to an adjacent mussel bed. A significant quantity of Late Iron Age pottery (dated between 100BC and AD43) was recorded nearby, together with burnt clay, bone and charcoal. The remains of at least one whale, and possibly a second, were recovered from within the channel, and one of them bore clear marks of butchery. This collection produced useful information about the social and economic life on the shingle, probably in the Late Iron Age. But so far no signs of permanent prehistoric habitation have been found.

All this evidence of prehistoric activity came from the crests of shingle ridges on the landward side of the Dungeness shingle mass. Fortunately, the geological survey already carried out in the area of the gravel extraction and its broader environment had provided information on the surroundings. Both the Bronze Age and the Late Iron Age people would have looked west from their shingle ridge out over a lower-lying salt marsh. It would have been a landscape of sandy channels and mudflats rising up to a platform of high salt marsh. Minor channels would have woven their sinuous courses through this high salt marsh, and not far to the west of the shingle barrier there may already have been one much wider channel, the forerunner of the *Wainway*, though this is not certain. The flow of the smaller, neap tides would have been limited to the channels and mudflats, but the twice-monthly spring tides would have covered the entire vegetated platform. In the other direction, away to the east, lay the sea — though that was becoming progressively more remote as the Dungeness promontory was built further and further out as increasing quantities of shingle arrived from the south-west.

This prompts the question as to how prehistoric men reached this area. It seems unlikely that they would have struggled and stumbled at least 9 miles (15km) along the surface of the bare shingle from the upland. Alternatively, they may have wended their way in flat-bottomed boats through the marsh channels, or at low tide in summer they could simply have walked across the salt marshes and forded the channels.

By 2,000 years ago the foundations for the Marsh were laid. That formation had involved two crucial steps. About 6,000 years ago the shingle barrier began to grow out from Fairlight across the great sandy bay, causing the tides to deposit fine-grained silt and clay in the shelter behind it. Then, around 3,000 years ago, rising sea level out-paced the upward growth of the Marsh and the tides began to flow higher, slowly but progressively advancing. Paradoxically, this 'drowning' initiated a build-up of further sediment, which was essential if it was ever to be possible for man to occupy and farm the Marsh. At the same time, waterlogged conditions further from the sea produced peat of considerable depth, which was to cause very considerable problems for those who attempted to drain the land many centuries later. The marsh was crossed by a branching pattern of numerous minor tidal channels, which joined up with a few major ones.

This frontier zone was certainly being used in the Early Bronze Age, though as far as we know at present, prehistoric occupation was limited to the back of the shingle barrier. But there may still be surprises in store. Archaeological observation will continue as gravel quarrying progresses, and post-excavation reports on laboratory work on samples already collected are eagerly awaited. The stage was set for the arrival of the Romans. In the past, they have been credited with great engineering works for keeping the sea out. But can these claims be justified?

3 The Roman enigma

Evidence of Roman activity on the Marsh is very limited. This is surprising because it is well known that the Romans had the technological skill necessary to drain and occupy marshland, as is shown by their extensive colonization of the silt belt in the East Anglian Fens. Secondly, the position of the Marsh in the frontier zone facing the Continent suggests that it might well have been an early candidate for reclamation. In addition to that, there is a well-established local legend that 'the Romans were the first to secure Romney Marsh from the sea'. So what is the reason for the apparent lack of evidence? Was the Marsh widely occupied but is the Roman land-surface buried so deeply beneath later sediments that the evidence has not come to light? Was, perhaps, the Marsh physically unsuitable for occupation? Or was it a cultural backwater that was ignored by the Romans?

Such evidence as there is of Roman occupation has emerged occasionally over the last two centuries, much of it by chance. The first and by all accounts the most spectacular discovery was made back in the 1840s when the sea was encroaching on the south-west end of the Dymchurch Wall and the wall was being rebuilt. When soil was removed from neighbouring fields to build up the new wall, an extensive area of occupation spread over several acres was uncovered well below high water mark (**14**). When the Rev S. Isaacson, curate of Dymchurch, reported the discovery to a meeting of the British Archaeological Association in Canterbury in September 1844, he speculated that the finds were connected with the 'invasion by Caesar and the settlement of the Romans in this country'. He also wrote that 'the appearance of the land indicates the existence at some remote period of extensive earthworks'. The finds included beautiful Samian (high-class ceramic) ware, fragments of several 'chastely designed' urns, mortars and whetstones, and large quantities of pottery. There were cinerary urns containing ashes of the dead, a cemetery, and bones of horse, boar and deer. There were also large quantities of ash and charcoal, and 'immense masses' of crude pieces of burnt clay 3-6in (7-15cm) long. Isaacson was clearly puzzled by this crude pottery, which he described as made by rolling a piece of clay in the hand and then striking each end against a board. More recently, however, it has been identified from his description as briquetage, which is very crude, very fragile pottery associated with extraction of salt from sea water. The Dymchurch discovery is therefore now interpreted primarily as a large-scale salt-working site. In 1845, when the sea was continuing to encroach, James Elliott, the engineer in charge of re-building the wall, took personal charge of the archaeological finds. None was retained locally, and as far as is known they were distributed between the British Museum, the Pitt Rivers Museum in Oxford and the Bateman Collection in Sheffield.

At that time there was an increasing interest in archaeology, and this discovery

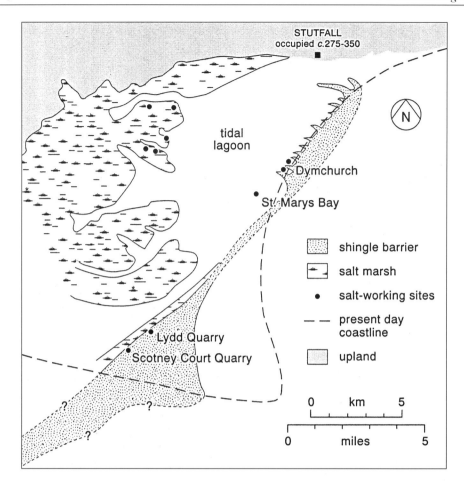

14 A conjectural map of Romney Marsh in c.AD100, showing the Roman salt-working sites round the edge of a tidal area. They were almost all overwhelmed by AD200 by the advancing sea. The fort of Stutfall was sited on this tidal inlet, over-looking the Marsh

provided a great stimulus to interest in the antiquity and archaeology of the Marsh. On the strength of it Elliott suggested, mistakenly as it turned out, that the original Dymchurch Wall had been built by the Romans. That idea gathered strength twenty years later when interest was roused still further by the excavation of the fort of *Stutfall*. Elliott was then encouraged to claim that the Romans had enclosed and reclaimed the whole of Romney Marsh proper by building both the Dymchurch Wall and the Rhee Wall, which runs from Appledore to Romney. This theory gripped public imagination at the time, and even now it appears in some publications. But it cannot be substantiated, and understanding of the timing of the reclamation of Romney Marsh proper is now very different.

More than 100 years later, further considerable evidence of a buried Roman land-surface came to light near the light railway station at St Mary's Bay during the systematic augering by the Soil Survey in the 1960s (**14**). This, found at depths between 15in (37cm) and 30in (75cm), was scattered with multicoloured pottery debris and charcoal. Half a mile (800m) further west, broken pottery, which was dated to the late first century BC or early first century AD was found at a similar depth together with a skeleton, probably that of a young horse. The sea had clearly invaded this Roman land-surface, as it had been cut into by a minor creek: a lump of the old surface was found among the sediments in the creek, having been broken off the side by an incoming tide. Shells collected from a similar creek one mile (1.6km) south of Old Romney were radiocarbon dated to AD400, indicating that silting of these creeks was well advanced by then.

In 1970, when a new drainage ditch was being cut in the north-west of the Marsh, another glass urn containing cremated bone fragments was found, neatly surrounded by two glass vessels dated between AD75 and 120 and two second-century Samian dishes. The group lay about 4ft (1.2m) below the present surface, and had evidently been buried as grave goods in honour of a person of considerable local importance (**colour plate 6**). More briquetage and pottery sherds of similar age have been discovered in the same general area, again from depths of about 3ft (1m), mostly only found when observant farmers were cleaning out ditches or drilling holes for fence-posts. In 1988 an extensive salt-working site was found during ditch-digging operations, and this was followed by other similar evidence (**14**). More pottery and coins have been found elsewhere, but none in sufficient concentrations for an occupied site or particular activity to be identified. Some of this came from depth, but a small amount of pottery has been reported on the surface.

In the 1990s exciting new horizons were opened up when gravel extraction operations west and south-west of Lydd area began to expose large areas of buried landscapes. When the Scotney Court gravel quarry next to the Camber Road some 2.5 miles (4km) south-west of Lydd was already nearly worked out, a pink layer of briquetage, pottery and charcoal was noticed on one face of a narrow causeway which still survived between two very large areas of water (**colour plate 7**). Both excavation and detailed post-excavation assessment were made possible by grants from the Romney Marsh Research Trust. This was evidently a salt-working site, and may have been on a large scale. But unfortunately when it was excavated no hearths were found and only one possible evaporation pan was discovered; it was therefore concluded that the area where those central activities had taken place had probably already been quarried away. The pottery was of Late Iron Age/Early Romano-British type, dated between AD25 and 100, and nearly all of it was simple and utilitarian. No Samian ware was found, a further confirmation that this was only a low-status site. Friable briquetage is so easily broken down that the surviving pieces were difficult to distinguish, but they included pedestals and crude cylindrical vessels probably used for evaporation or storage of the salt.

Because this was, rather amazingly, the first Roman site to be properly excavated on the Marsh, special attention was paid to a detailed environmental investigation. The charcoal — the fuel used for heating the brine — came mainly from oak and pine, species of the upland rather than the marshes, and so had apparently been brought down to the Marsh to support the salt industry. Domestic rubbish included a small assemblage of bones, more from cows than sheep, some of which showed signs of butchery, and a few pigs. A small collection of fish bones was also recovered, in which halibut and cod or haddock were identified. Two of those specimens bore evidence that suggested fish may have been salted at the site before being sent inland, or even abroad.

A localised lens of shingle showed that part of the site had been overrun by the sea sometime in the first century. Salt-working had resumed after that event, but there was no indication that it continued into the second century. The Roman layer had been sealed in by a layer of shingle that contained rolled briquetage, proving that at some later date the sea had once again flooded the site. However, the fact that the friable briquetage had survived at all provided a further clue. The inundation must have taken place in very calm conditions, because no briquetage could have survived buffeting by more than a couple of waves on a beach exposed to the open sea.

After the Scotney Court quarry closed, gravel-working transferred to Lydd Quarry, 1.25 miles (2km) nearer Lydd, extracting shingle ridges which geographers recognised as being approximately the same age as those at Scotney Court. By then Dr John Williams had been appointed as the first County Archaeological Officer for Kent and the planning permission was given on condition that funds were provided by the developer, Robert Brett and Sons Limited, for archaeological assessment of the area. A second-century cremation urn was recovered very early on during topsoil stripping of the plant site, but despite a careful search of the surrounding area no further burials were found. A large quantity of Romano-British pottery was found nearby, lying in a dark layer of sandy silt in a hollow in the surface of a shingle ridge. This suggested that the dark Roman horizon had previously been more widespread but that the evidence had unfortunately been destroyed by later ploughing. Also, the pottery bore signs of having been rounded off, which implied that it had been washed in with pebbles from some other nearby site when the sea broke over the workings. The pottery was mainly from the first and second century AD with only a small quantity from early in the third, and there was nothing to suggest that occupation continued after that.

In 1996 a large quantity of second-century pottery was found covering an area approximately 24ft (7m) in each direction, lying above the Bronze Age occupation layer already described on page 39. Finds included pieces of coarse-ware jars, bowls or platters, and lids, and also five Samian sherds. As at the 1991 site, the upper part of the Roman occupation layer had unfortunately been lost to later ploughing. The silty infilling of a local channel contained fragments of whale bone, showing that one or possibly two animals had been stranded nearby and then been butchered. A nearby area of rippled marine sand contained more second-century pottery which had apparently been re-worked when the sea had flooded the site. Again, there was no evidence of occupation later than early third century — or indeed that it resumed before the late twelfth century. Sometime in the interim the sea had advanced again and covered the whole area with a deep layer of yellowish brown silty clay.

Both these excavated sites had been flooded occasionally, which suggests that life on the shingle barrier was uncertain, and sometimes downright unsafe. It would have been a very uncomfortable place to be at times when the water in the salt marshes on the landward side was raised by a storm surge, and the only way back to the security of the upland was by boat over those choppy waters or a 10 mile (16km) struggle back along the barrier to Pett.

Professor Barry Cunliffe had already provided, in 1980, a cultural explanation for the apparently limited occupation of the Marsh. He pointed out that in the late Iron Age the Weald and most of the South Downs had been cut off from the main centres of innovation, which were around the Thames and other rivers flowing into the North Sea, and around the Solent. In the period of Romanization after AD43 urban centres and road systems developed, but they were based on the late Iron Age socio-economic pattern. No Roman centre developed in the south-east coastal zone between Chichester and Canterbury, and as far as the Marsh was concerned little changed from the pre-Roman era. It remained a cultural backwater where local resources, especially salt, were exploited as part of a strictly local economy. In the absence of well-recorded excavated sites it was impossible for Cunliffe to assess the nature of any settlements or their economies, but in 1988 he suggested the following model. The sites were summer camps occupied by a population who came down to the Marsh on a seasonal basis. Those people extracted salt from sea water, concentrated the brine over fires (hence the briquetage), and at the same time pastured their flocks on the lush salt-marsh vegetation. They may have stayed till early autumn when fattened stock were killed off and salted down and the leather was processed using the salt. In winter, when it was impossible to evaporate the salt and the tides were more likely to overflow temporarily both salt-extraction sites and pasture, they retreated to more permanent settlements on the upland. The recent excavations near Lydd have served to confirm this model, and the quantity and quality of pottery found there indicates that largish groups of people were involved, and they came to the Marsh for considerable periods rather than just the odd week.

The picture which has emerged from the archaeological record so far confirms that the Roman land-surface is generally buried beneath a metre or so of later sediments. Hence it is very difficult to assess in any detail except where it has been exposed by quarrying, and even there it is not easy. Relatively few pottery sherds have come from the surface, and they seem at present to be 'odd men out'. Little can be concluded from them without detailed 'keyhole' excavation and equally detailed mapping of the buried land-surface, which might possibly prove that those places remained as islands during the subsequent inundation. Until that has been done, the suspicion remains that those sherds had probably been brought up by the plough.

The position and nature of the sites is highly significant (*see* **14**). They are scattered round the fringe of Romney Marsh proper, either just on the edge of the salt-marsh peat as mapped by the Soil Survey, or close behind the back of the shingle barrier. Most were connected to the production of salt, an almost essential commodity used for preserving meat and fish, curing hides and flavouring cereals. A glance at present day salt production helps to explain this distribution. For instance, in the Baie de Bourgneuf on the French Atlantic coast, salt-making takes place only at sites adjacent to tidal creeks high up on the salt marshes. Salt water is taken in only at spring tides. This not only explains why the Romney Marsh sites are found round the fringe of the area, but also serves to confirm the geographers' understanding that salt-marsh conditions never extended out over the centre of Romney Marsh proper. That area must have always remained sand and mudflats covered twice-daily by the tides.

The sites had apparently all been abandoned by AD200, or in the case of the shingle barrier only slightly later, due to a steady advance of the sea. The geologists explain that from 1200BC the sea had been slowly advancing and the water table rising. Some of the effects have already been picked up by the archaeologists. The sites on the shingle barrier were washed over from time to time and the artefacts rolled about, and the tides evidently advanced with some force up a creek near St Mary in the Marsh. Then, it seems, a critical level was reached towards the end of the second century and most of the salt-marsh platform became flooded by high tides. The scene must have resembled present conditions on the submerged forest outside the sea wall at Pett Level, where the incoming tides cover the peat beds very quickly. There, a platform of peat rests on blue clay, a variety of useless logs litter the surface, and the whole surface is often covered by a veneer of silt which makes it so slippery that it is very difficult to stand up (**colour plate 5**). It is altogether a most inhospitable environment. With their sites and pastures flooded, and salt-making no longer an option, it is hardly surprising that the inhabitants abandoned the Marsh and retreated to the upland, as far as those individuals were concerned, forever.

Even if it had still been physically possible to continue to occupy the Marsh, life on the south-east coast was soon to become insecure for another reason. The timing is very uncertain, but at least from the third century barbarian tribesman from beyond the borders of the Roman Empire swept down on Germany, Gaul and on the east coast of Britain. Groups of people best described as pirates or raiders crossed the Channel and attempted to slip inland, up the estuaries and inlets. The Roman response in the mid-third century was to build a chain of massive forts extending from Brancaster in north Norfolk to Portchester on Chichester Harbour, each of them in a strategic position guarding an inlet.

The forts are known collectively as the Forts of the Saxon Shore because, according to the *Notitia Dignitatum*, which gives full details of the commands and postings of all the troops in the Roman world in *c*.400, they were commanded by the Count of the Saxon Shore. Otherwise no documentation about them has survived, and it is not even clear whether the Saxons were the attackers or were already employed by the Romans as mercenaries to man the forts. In addition, the *Notitia* also lists a string of names of coastal fortifications in Gaul, one of which has been excavated at Oudenburg, near Bruges. This has prompted the suggestion that there may have been some kind of system of trans-Channel cooperation, attempting to frustrate the pirates by allowing them to sail south through the Strait of Dover and then cutting off their retreat to the North Sea.

Stutfall, which lies slumped in ruins overlooking Romney Marsh on the northern hills below Lympne Castle, was one of these forts, its nearest neighbours in the chain being at Dover to the north-east and Pevensey to the south-west (**colour plate 8**). The hill is capped by Hythe Beds, a limestone otherwise known as the Kentish Ragstone, and the slopes below are formed in the Weald Clay. The limestone was used to build the fort, and the clay was responsible for the substantial landslips that destroyed it. The site is now a delightfully peaceful spot off the beaten track, and is some 1.5 miles (2.5km) from the sea. In the third century, however, it was of considerable strategic importance, guarding the entrance to the large Romney Marsh inlet which offered a sheltered haven for shipping very near the shortest Channel crossing (*see* **14**). For 75 years, and possibly more, that hillside was the focus of intense activity.

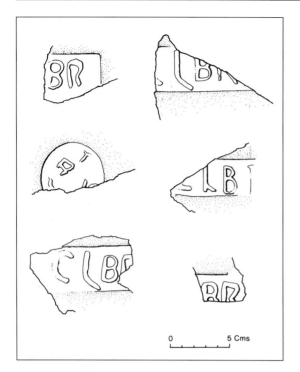

15 Earlier artefacts built, second-hand, into the c.275 fort of Stutfall:
  (left) Tiles stamped CL BR, for Classis Britannica
  (right) An altar to Neptune set up by Aufridus Pantera, the prefect of the Classis Britannica

Although the fort we see today was built in *c.*270-80, and abandoned around 350, there is a strong suspicion that there may have been an earlier fort nearby. There are several reasons for this. Earlier artefacts have been found built into the present structure. Tiles stamped with CL BR are indicative of a local association with the Roman fleet (the *Classis Britannica*) and possibly with the Wealden iron industry, which must have been not later than the end of the second century. An altar dedicated to Neptune set up by Aufridus Pantera, the prefect of the *Classis Britannica* at an earlier date, had found its way into an unexpectedly lowly setting — the foundations of the east gate (**15**, *see* also **17**). One coin of similar date was also found. In addition, this area had good connections with the wider world early in the Roman period, for Lympne was connected with Canterbury by road, and another road ran west along the Kentish Ragstone ridge towards London. As well as that, the *Antonine Itinerary* refers to a *Portus Lemanis* in the early third century. All this suggests that there may well have been an earlier fort in the area although, despite repeated searches, no early building has yet been found. It is not impossible that one remains hidden beneath the landslips.

The fort we see today was first excavated by Charles Roach Smith and James Elliott (the engineer in charge of the Dymchurch Wall) in 1850, then by Sir Victor Horsley in 1893-94, and by Professor Barry Cunliffe in three seasons from 1976 to 1978. In 1981-82

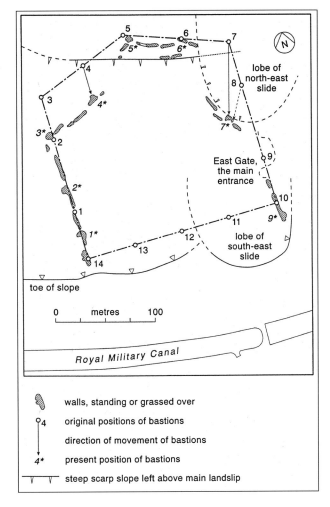

16 A reconstructed plan of Roman fort of Stutfall, showing the three landslips which affected it. Very little of the masonry is in its original position. Compare this to **colour plate 8**. After Hutchinson et al. 1985

Professor John Hutchinson led a geotechnical investigation into the effects of the landslips on the fort.

An area of some 4 acres (1.6ha) was enclosed by massive curtain walls with bastions at regular intervals. The walls were 12ft (3.65m) thick, with a core of Kentish Ragstone rubble, faced inside and outside with squared-off ashlar blocks of the ragstone, and with characteristic layers of red tiles laid at regular intervals between the courses of ashlar. Most of the ragstone blocks were robbed away long ago, since they served as a ready-made quarry for medieval buildings, including Lympne Church and Castle on the crest of the hill above. The structure was, however, wrecked by landslips and has been further obscured by soil moving down the hill, so that although very substantial ruins remain, very little is in its original position (**16**). Three main landslips affected it. The most violent of these took place in the north-east corner, no doubt related to a large stream which comes down the hill. Another slip occurred in the south-east, dislocating the east gate and pushing a prominent lobe of the hillside out on to the marsh. The gate had originally been flanked by two bastions: the upper one had disintegrated, and the lower one had been

17 The east gate of
Stutfall excavated in
1976. The lower
bastion, in the
foreground, is faced
with six courses of
blocks of Kentish
Ragstone, above
which traces of a
characteristic course of
(red) Roman tiles can
be picked out. A
landslip tilted this
bastion in towards the
centre of the fort, and
was responsible for
the destruction of the
upper bastion in the
background

tilted at a sharp angle inwards (**17**). The substantial base of the gate, built of large stone blocks, had been broken into thirteen fragments.

A third landslip was responsible for the collapse of the north walls. Trenches cut in 1981 slightly upslope from the remains of the north walls produced spectacular results, showing that the Romans were well aware of the problems they faced in building on an unstable hillside. They had dug a foundation trench about 1.5m deep, and then driven closely-spaced short oak piles down into the Weald Clay — a not uncommon Roman practice when building on unstable ground. A platform of rough ragstone was then packed round the top of the piles to provide a working surface for the construction of the foundations and the wall. The story of the collapse of the wall unfolded in two of the trenches. Some of the oak piles had been bent when the wall collapsed. Those in one trench were now horizontal, and in the other they were also bent over at an angle (**18**). Above them, a trail of ragstone debris headed down the hill, above which was a shear-plane.

The wall had collapsed because the main landslip had removed the supporting ground from the lower side of it, while a mass of soil (colluvium) had built up against the upper side (**19**). It had slid downhill, bending the top of some of the piles as it went, and leaving a trail of debris behind it. Bastion 5 had moved about 16ft (5m) downhill, while Bastion 6 moved only about 4ft (1.2m). Finally the wall tipped over, coming to rest at an angle between 22° and 28°. By establishing the original position of the northern walls,

18 A trench cut into the landslips above the present position of the north walls of Stutfall. *This shows the dark oak piles driven by the Romans into the shiny Weald Clay. Those in the foreground are approximately vertical, those further away were bent downhill (obliquely right) at an angle of 30° when the wall slid off its foundations. The scale is marked off in 10cm lengths*

Hutchinson was also able to prove that the fort had originally been five-sided, with two upslope walls meeting at an obtuse angle at Bastion 6.

No trace of the south wall of the fort survives on the surface, but it was found when two trenches were dug through the lobe of the south-east landslip and out on to the Marsh. At the same time an important relationship was established between the relative timing of the landslips and the accumulation of sediment brought into the inlet by the sea. At the bottom of the trenches a thick beach deposit of sand and shingle was found, and was clearly Roman or post-Roman because it contained a fragment of red tile. Above that was 6ft (2m) of grey marine silt, and while that was accumulating, the clay ground on which the wall had been built slipped downhill and the wall toppled over. Three feet (1m) of the grey silt was deposited after the wall collapsed. It has not been possible to establish the date of the landslides that destroyed the fort, which is unfortunate because if that were known it would be an indication of the date of silting of the inlet. But at least it is clear that the sea had access to the area for some time afterwards. The fort itself was abandoned, for an unknown reason, in *c.*350, some decades earlier than the other Forts of the Saxon Shore. But it had the distinction of remaining by far the largest structure on or overlooking the Marsh until the nuclear power stations were built at Dungeness in the 1960s and '70s.

To sum up, some aspects of the Roman enigma can now be satisfactorily explained.

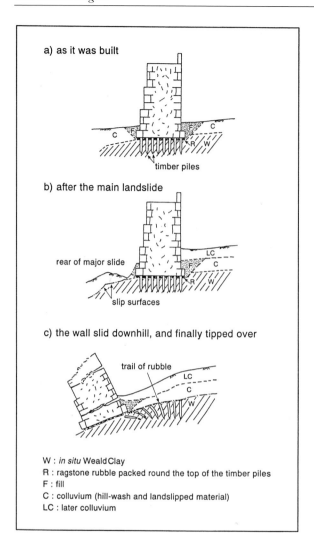

a) as it was built

timber piles

b) after the main landslide

rear of major slide

slip surfaces

c) the wall slid downhill, and finally tipped over

trail of rubble

W : *in situ* Weald Clay
R : ragstone rubble packed round the top of the timber piles
F : fill
C : colluvium (hill-wash and landslipped material)
LC : later colluvium

19 Three stages in the collapse of the north wall of Stutfall. Discovery of the piles sunk to support the wall made it possible to measure how far it had moved downhill. Based on Hutchinson et al. *1985*

The Roman land-surface generally lies beneath a metre of later sediments, which are almost certain to be obscuring more evidence of occupation. But the geological and archaeological evidence combine to give a strong indication that the central area of Romney Marsh proper remained tidal sand and mudflats throughout the Roman period, and therefore was not likely to have been suitable for either occupation or reclamation. In other words, Romney Marsh offered no equivalent to the silt belt which was occupied in the Fens of East Anglia at that time. It also seems that the south-east corner of the country between Chichester and Canterbury was by-passed by Roman civilisation. Moreover, the sea was advancing and by the end of the second century had overrun even the salt-working sites. It thus seems clear that by the mid-fourth century both the Marsh and the fort overlooking it had been deserted.

4 The Saxon imprint

In striking contrast to the limited evidence of Roman occupation, and lack of it after *c*.200, the Domesday Book (1086) and Domesday Monachorum (a parallel but slightly different record of the monks of Christ Church Canterbury) together show that by *c*.1100 most of Romney Marsh proper (an area of over 24,000 acres or 10,000ha) was occupied on a year-round basis. So was a large area of Denge Marsh, and relatively large settlements had grown up at Romney and Lydd (*see* **1**). For the first time the sea had been excluded from a large part of the present land area. This chapter explores how and why these large tidal areas had become dry land suitable for permanent settlement, and when they were colonised.

The late Roman/early Saxon time presents an excellent illustration of an important paradox of marshland reclamation and settlement. When the sea floods in over the marsh and the inhabitants have to retreat, the situation seems disastrous in human terms. On the other hand, a prolonged inundation is extremely beneficial for future generations, because every incoming tide deposits a load of sediment. In this way areas which are flooded by the sea are built up and in due course become higher, better drained and are more desirable land. Conversely, those areas which the tides do not reach are destined to remain relatively low-lying, liable to flooding, difficult to drain, and generally much less valuable.

When the sea overwhelmed the marsh in later Roman times it deposited new layers of sediment. A new salt marsh developed (but was not preserved as peat this time, because it was never sealed in by another layer of sediment). The tides did not, however, often reach right across the marsh, and therefore the soils above the peat become thinner further away from the open sea. By the time the Appledore Dowels (north-east of Appledore) and the area between Fairfield and The Cheyne are reached the peat is within 1ft (30cm) of the surface, so that logs and the roots of trees in it can be seen in the side of the ditches (**20**). These places were evidently near the limit of the tides flowing in round the northern point of the shingle barrier.

In quite a short space of time the rate of sedimentation on this new marsh must have exceeded that of the rise in sea level, and the tides became restricted to the creeks. The general marsh plateau was seldom overflowed, and its well-vegetated surface would have been available for summer grazing. Soon after that the creeks silted up and the land could be occupied permanently.

The sinuous creeks were by far the most important element of the new landscape, because the silt was dug out and they were used as the freshwater drainage channels. Also, silt and vegetation had to be repeatedly cleared out of the watercourses and was dumped alongside, thus providing banks that were marginally higher and drier than the general marsh surface. Those banks were then used as causeways for getting about the Marsh and, many centuries later, some were upgraded to become the tarmac roads of today. The

20 A three-thousand-year-old log projecting from the side of a sewer in the Appledore Dowels. The causeway in the background carries the Ashford-Rye railway, and owing to the considerable thickness of peat near the surface, the ground 'quakes' whenever a train passes

sinuous pattern of salt-marsh creeks is stamped on the watercourses and roads all over Romney Marsh proper, as a quick glance at an Ordnance Survey map will show. This explains why, as local people know only too well, most of the roads of Romney Marsh proper follow winding, wandering routes. Because they were difficult for both humans and their animals to cross, the deep steep-sided creeks also became property boundaries. Initially they were used as the boundaries of the great Saxon estates, some of which were adopted as the parish boundaries from the ninth century onwards.

Thus the landscape of today is based on the features of a late Roman/early Saxon salt marsh. Over the centuries the framework has been adapted to suit economic and social needs or adjusted according to local requirements of land drainage, but these did not change that basic framework. As far as we know, there is no relationship between the sites occupied in the Saxon period and those previously occupied by the Romans.

A remarkable survival of documentary material provides some indication of when this colonisation took place. Of all the early kingdoms which evolved during the Anglo-Saxon period, Kent has by far the largest number of charters surviving from the seventh and eighth centuries, some of which refer to Romney Marsh. These documents recorded grants of land, mostly from the king to ecclesiastical bodies or lay landlords. They show something of how owners originally secured their hold on the land, and explain why, later on, the monasteries were the principal landowners in the medieval period. They also show, very usefully, that certain estates actually existed and were dry land by particular dates.

Most of the Romney Marsh charters deal with the transfer of blocks of land to the double minster of Lyminge (a community of itinerant priests who served a wide area, and nuns), which stood on the chalk Downs to the north. Their remarkable survival over some twelve hundred years is due to a series of fortunate accidents. The minister declined sometime in the ninth or tenth centuries, possibly as a result of Viking disturbances, and its lands and associated documents were then transferred to the priory of Christ Church Canterbury. At the Dissolution of the priory in *c*.1540 the documents were put into the safe keeping of the Dean and Chapter, the body which administers the cathedral. Apart from being temporarily removed to London during the Civil War, they have rested in the cathedral archives ever since. Other documents concerned land in the Burmarsh area belonging to St Augustine's Abbey, Canterbury.

The charters were translated, and the estates they describe identified on the map, by Dr Gordon Ward, the antiquarian from Sevenoaks, in the 1930s. The earliest charter, dated *c*.700, is a good example:

> In the name of Our Lord Jesus Christ. I, Whitred, king of the men of Kent, having my future in mind, have decided to give away something of all that has been given to me. After taking counsel, it has seemed good to give to the church of the Blessed Mary, the Mother of God, which is situated in a place called Lyminge, the land of four ploughs which is called *Pleghelmestun* . . . Also I grant to be possessed for ever by the same mother of God, Blessed Mary, a little land called *Rumining seta*, for the pasture of 300 sheep. This is on the south side of the river *Limenea* but we do not set down the boundaries because they are well known to the countryfolk all round . . . (**21**).

21 *The* Rumining seta *charter of c.696, by which Whitred, king of Kent, gave that area of pasture near Dymchurch to the double minster at Lyminge*

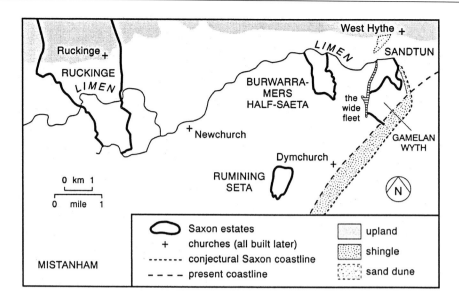

22 Saxon estates on the Marsh and the northern Limen *channel. Most of these estates were mapped on the basis of Saxon charters by Dr Gordon Ward. Dr Nicholas Brooks then drew in the course of the* Limen, *based on the Soil Survey map. The boundaries of* Sandtun *and* Mistanham *(later Misleham) have never been defined*

The name *Pleghelmestun* referred to *Wilmington*, an estate on the upland which was merged with the manor of Sellindge before the Conquest, but it is the relatively small *Rumining seta*, the Romney enclosure, which is of special interest to us. This was the detached portion of Sellindge parish (as it was before late Victorian rationalisation of the parish boundaries) where the name still survives in Sellinge Farm, a little way inland from Dymchurch (**22**). It was not uncommon at this early date for manors on the upland to have sheep pastures on the Marsh, and here we have confirmation that an upland community based some 6 miles (9km) away, was pasturing a nominal number of 300 sheep near Dymchurch. It is quite possible that transhumance was being practised and the sheep, liable to foot-rot and liver fluke on wet pastures in the winter, were being brought down to the marsh for the summer. The route they took to get to the Dymchurch area remains an interesting open question: they must have had to cross the *Limen*, a watercourse that is discussed below.

Another group of charters describes an estate in Ruckinge parish in the north-west of the Marsh. When this was granted to Lyminge in 734 it was said to have previously belonged to Ickham, east of Canterbury. Here, then, was another estate that had once belonged to a community based some 20 miles (38km) away. It was cut in two by the *Limen* watercourse, which Ward correctly identified with the bold curves of the Sedbrook Sewer (**22**).

Several other charters dealt with estates in the north-east. In *c.*845 the *Limen* formed the northern boundary of a large estate, *Burwaramers half-saeta,* a line which is still the boundary of Burmarsh parish. A neighbouring estate of *Gamelanwyth*, granted to two brothers by King Edmund in a charter dated 946, lay to the east, on the other side of a wide fleet and watercourse which became the boundary between Dymchurch, Burmarsh and West Hythe parishes and is still visible as a wide trough in the landscape. That estate extended eastwards as far as a shingle bank — beyond which was the sea (**22**). Evidently some, at least, of the parish boundaries are those of the Saxon estates and are of great antiquity.

All these charters refer to land in the north-east of the Marsh as a whole. There is a strong probability that, because the soils above the peat become thinner towards the south-west, the deeper, better-drained soils were colonised first. The only charter which can be identified with any certainty in the south-west refers to *Mistanham*, whose name survives in Misleham House 0.6 miles (1km) north of Brookland, which had the advantage of being on the side of a broad sandy creek ridge. It was given directly to Christ Church Priory by King Æthelwulf of Kent at some date between 833 and 858 (*see* page 69).

These surviving documents describe only a few widely-spaced estates, but they must be representative of many more similar estates for which the documents have long since been lost or destroyed. Indeed, the Sellinge charter implies that the *Rumining seta* was surrounded by similar land when it states 'the boundaries . . . are well known to the country folk all around'. Although this record is very fragmentary, it seems safe to assume that a large part of Romney Marsh proper had become dry land and was occupied in the seventh and eighth centuries. It is, in addition, supported by finds of pottery sherds of the eighth to tenth centuries on the surface around Newchurch and Eastbridge. Certainly in 796 the Marsh was a well-recognised land area, since the *Anglo-Saxon Chronicle* tells us that in that year Coenwulf king of Mercia laid waste to 'the people of Kent and of the Marsh'. It was a battleground again in 838 when 'Herebryht the alderman was killed by heathen men (the Vikings) and many men with him in the Marsh'.

Lyminge and its itinerant priests were superseded between the ninth and eleventh centuries by local parish churches. Each of these was founded by the local landlord. His estate paid tithes to that church, and thus the estate became its parish. Some of them were named after those landlords. For instance, Orgarswick (*wic* often implied a remote farm with a specialist function, possibly sheep) and its church *Orgarescirce* were probably named after a man called Ordgar. Blackmanstone was named after Blaceman who held that land in the time of Edward the Confessor, which shows it was not founded until the mid-eleventh century. Dymchurch was *Demancirce*, named after *dema*, a judge. Otherwise, it is not known when Newchurch was 'new', but it was the centre of a 'hundred' recorded in Domesday Book. Eastbridge presumably refers to an important crossing over the *Limen*.

Domesday Book and Domesday Monachorum together provide the first overall survey of the area. They show that all the parish churches on Romney Marsh proper except for Snave and Snargate were in existence by 1100, though presumably as wooden buildings only later rebuilt in stone. Most of the churches of Romney Marsh proper, for example Burmarsh, Eastbridge, Newchurch, Snave and Blackmanstone, were built near the centre of their parish, and were clearly established after the marsh had already been colonised. As we shall see later, this stands out in marked contrast to the pattern of parish boundaries on Walland Marsh, where the parishes accumulated land in a very different fashion.

23 The Sandtun dune in 1947. This gives an impression of a very isolated site, but note the proximity to the Lympne escarpment in the background, from which people could easily have come down to trade and fish

The written documents provide a general idea of the date by which the sea retreated from Romney Marsh proper, but only archaeological investigation could provide information about the cultural life of that time. In 1931 Dr Gordon Ward identified a low sand dune on the north side of the *Limen* near West Hythe as being part of the estate of *Sandtun* (**22**, **23**). In 1940 Roman archaeological evidence was found there. This almost coincided with the discovery in 1939 of a Saxon warrior buried with fabulous gold and silver grave goods in a 90ft (27m) long ship at Sutton Hoo near Woodbridge, Suffolk. Interest and excitement became sharply focused on the potential of Saxon sites on sand dunes. Each one might be an Eldorado. There were, after all, important similarities between Sutton Hoo and *Sandtun*. Both were situated on sandy soils beside tidal inlets on the east coast. Surely something similar to Sutton Hoo might be found at *Sandtun*?

Ward had already translated two charters. In 732 King Æthelbert of Kent confirmed an earlier grant to Lyminge of an area of land 'suitable for a salt works', together with another 100 acres at *Sandtun*. The second charter, dated 833, made it clear that the salt works were by then in existence and that the estate had grown to 150 acres. The grants also included wood, probably from nearby *Saltwood*, 'for roasting the salt' (evaporating the brine). Aware that the site had exciting potential, in the summer of 1947 Ward (albeit not an archaeologist) conducted a two-week excavation with Major J.P.T. Birchell of the British Museum, which funded the excavation (**24**). But, unfortunately, because of a subsequent life-long disagreement between the two men, the excavation was never written up. Sketchy written records, photographs and field notes were moved from place to place and

24 The 1947
    excavation at
    Sandtun.
    The sloping
    nature of the
    mussel-rich
    layers can be
    seen

eventually became distributed between the British Museum and museums at Maidstone and Hythe.

In the 1990s archaeological investigation resumed in advance of planning permission for houses to be built on the site. But by then it had been very much damaged by wartime activities and sand quarrying, and by later use for demolition and as a pig and chicken farm. Very patient detective work was required to bring all the old records together with the small amount of information that could still be obtained by excavation.

Beneath the dune were several Roman beach ridges of pebbles mixed with clean yellow beach sand. This beach could not be later than the second century because it contained water-rolled Roman tiles (another indication that there may have been an early Roman fort in the *Stutfall*-West Hythe area). After a hiatus of several centuries, the next event was the development of the *Sandtun* dune early in the eighth century. Sand was blown up from the foreshore to the south-east and came to rest on the solid base of the shingle ridges. A thin dark layer of wind-blown sand was succeeded by a succession of dune-bedded, even dirtier layers each containing mussel shells. Perhaps surprisingly in view of the potential discomfort, it was while the sand was blowing up that the site was occupied. The wind-blown sand contained large quantities of fish bones and fish-hooks, and also pottery and coins. The pottery included a considerable quantity of north French and other foreign wares. There was one *sceat* (the earliest Anglo-Saxon English silver coin) dating from the 690s, one coin of Pepin the Short, father of Charlemagne, dated from the 780s, one coin of King Eadberht Praen (796-98) and four silver pennies of Coenwulf of Mercia (796-?821). On the basis of the pottery, the lower occupation layer is tentatively dated between *c*.690 and *c*.775, and the mussel-rich layers up to *c*.840. Regrettably no archaeological evidence of salt-making was found.

So what was going on at this site which must have been plagued by blown sand? Both the pottery and the coins show that it was, at least temporarily, more than just a coastal fishing camp. One suggestion is that local fishermen were crossing the Channel, entering French ports and bringing back local products, but that is not sufficient to explain the considerable quantity of foreign wares, nor the coin of Pepin the Short. It is more likely that it was a small, seasonal, trading centre. Its importance lies in the fact that it is the first site on the south and east coasts identified as trading with the Continent which was not a permanent settlement, and which was not evidently under royal control. It stands out in marked contrast with the larger, official trading centres at Southampton, London, Ipswich and York, where trading was under strict control of the kings.

The attraction of the site was the raised bank on which ships could be pulled up out of the reach of the Channel tides, in a sheltered tidal inlet near the shortest Channel crossing. It may have been visited once a summer by itinerant traders from the Continent. News that they had arrived would have spread quickly round the locality, people would have arrived from the upland and, for perhaps just a few days each year, *Sandtun* would have been a scene of bustle and excitement. Otherwise, because no permanent occupation site has been found, it was probably used as a base for fishing on a daily basis. It was, however, short-lived. Occupation had come to an end by the mid-ninth century. This was the time when Viking raids were intensifying. Coastal sites became unsafe, and the raids may well have put an end to all trading activities. It is also likely that, coincidentally, the inlet was silting up and it was no longer possible for ships to reach the dune.

The dune extended nearly halfway across the inlet and holds a key to understanding and dating the closure of the tidal inlet. It appears that the sea had retreated from Romney Marsh proper remarkably quickly early in the Saxon period. The silting process would naturally have gathered momentum. As the tidal area was reduced and less water flowed in, there was less to ebb away and scour the silt out of the channels. Sand began blowing onto *Sandtun* off the foreshore around 700, showing that the sea had already retreated, exposing sandflats to the wind. It seems that the ninth-century layers were sealed in by a small quantity of further sand, but then the sand-blow ceased, which suggests that the sandflats themselves had dried out and been reclaimed at that date. On the other hand the salt-working taking place in 833 shows that tidal water was still reaching some part of *Sandtun* at that time.

While the Hythe inlet was silting up, an immensely important development took place further south along the coast. The shingle barrier was breached, and a new inlet formed in the neighbourhood of Romney. The timing of this is uncertain. We only know that it had occurred some time before 741, for a charter shows that by then there was a small fishing settlement at the mouth of a watercourse which, most confusingly, had the same name as that across the north of the Marsh. King Æthelbert of Kent granted to the minster at Lyminge, 'his fishery which is at the mouth of the river whose name is *Limen*, and part of the field in which the oratory of St Martin is situate, and the fishermen's houses, and the fourth part of a ploughland about the same place.'

The name of Romney does not appear in the charter. The only means of identifying the location is the oratory dedicated to St Martin. We can only assume that this was the precursor of the larger medieval church, the only one on the Marsh with that dedication, which stood in New Romney until pulled down in the sixteenth century. The site of that remains as open amenity land on the north-east side of Ashford Road near the centre of the town (*see* **33**). It is not difficult to visualise the early settlement as a row, or maybe parallel rows, of fishermen's huts running down to the sea on that conveniently raised shingle bank, with nets hung out to dry between them — similar to the early settlement at Great Yarmouth and many other fishing villages the world over. Another charter, dated *c*.914, referred to a channel then known as the *Rumenesea* which reached the sea at Romney, and not long afterwards that name was adapted for the settlement itself.

Thus Romney originated as a fishing settlement. Very little is known of its early history: it was one of a number of small ports along the south-east coast. But by the mid-eleventh century Romney had come to the fore as one of the Cinque Ports, as they were to become. No doubt this was due to its excellent natural haven. By the time of Edward the Confessor (1042-66) it had a mint. The economic importance of the haven was matched by the strategic value of its ships and crews, who were liable to be pressed into military service by the Crown. In 1052, during skirmishes between the massed forces of Saxon warlords, Earl Godwin and his son Harold sailed east along the south coast, seizing all the ships they could find in several ports, which included Romney. The chronicle of William of Poitiers describes how immediately after the Battle of Hastings William of Normandy secured Romney on his way to Dover. He took the opportunity to punish the men of Romney for killing some Normans who had landed there after being separated from the main fleet.

Further south again, Lydd church is the only one on the Marsh to include some pre-Conquest stonework. The north-west corner of the nave incorporates part of the structure of an early basilica, which had a 26ft (7.9m)-long nave, two aisles, a semi-circular apse in the east and a door at the west end.

Two charters show that a large area of Denge Marsh, lying in the shelter of shingle banks south of Lydd, was also dry land. The grant given by King Æthelbert to Lyminge in 741 included 'grazing for 150 cattle next to the marsh called Bishop's Wic, as far as the wood called ripp . . . and the bounds of Sussex', which had previously belonged to Romanus, a priest. Ward identified this with the Midrips area, south-west of Lydd. The other, which is only a tenth-century copy of a grant alleged to date from 774, referred to three sulungs (a large area) of land bounded on the north-west by *Bleccing*, north-east of Scotney Court, and extending as far as 'the stone situated at the end of the land', a picturesque description of an early equivalent of Greatstone, the outermost shingle ridge of the Dungeness complex. To the north and east of this lay the sea.

The subject of a possible course of the Rother across the Marsh has been shrouded in confusion since Ward identified what were evidently two different *Limen* channels. One of these lay across the north of the Marsh and reached the sea near Hythe (*see* **22**). He was clearly puzzled as to whether it was, or was not, a river, referring to it at one point as 'small and un-riverly'! He probably did not realise that the word *Limen* could be applied to other watercourses besides a freshwater river. We now understand that the name could have referred simply to a salt-marsh channel filled twice a day by the tides. In the north-east

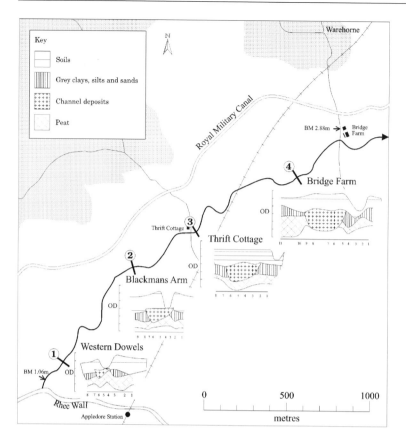

25 Not the 'northern course of the Rother'

only, it was large enough to be a property boundary, or at least a serious obstacle to human passage. The problem of whether or not it had been a river, containing a significant amount of fresh water, could only be solved by detailed geological investigation of the channel and the sediments filling it. This was carried out in 1987, and showed that the channel between Warehorne and Appledore Station bore no resemblance to the known seventeenth-century channel of the Rother at Smallhythe, being very much narrower and shallower. Also the grain-size of the sediments and microfauna contained in them were characteristic of tidal rather than fluvial conditions (**25**). This showed, therefore, that this part of the *Limen* was simply the upper reaches of a tidal creek, and could never have been the Rother.

Ward's vision of a second *Limen* appeared in his last paper, published in 1952. This channel swept south from the Isle of Oxney to a 'Great Marsh near Rye' and then east and north, to find its way to the sea leaving both Old and New Romney on the north bank. He definitely thought that this contained the Rother. Although it is not clear what gave him this idea, the seaward end fits amazingly well with the broad and deep sandy channel proved recently by the scientists, and with the *Wainway* as shown on the maps of *c.*1600 (**26**, *see* also **57** and **colour plate 25**).

R.D. Green of the Soil Survey suggested yet another possible 'river' course, a sinuous channel which he identified running north of and parallel to the Rhee, from Snargate to

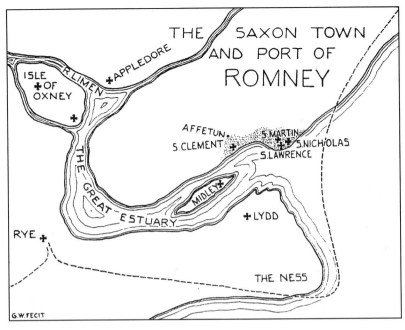

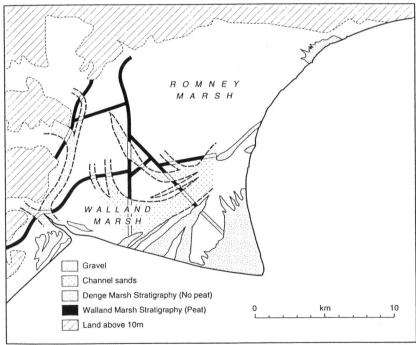

26 Two maps of the Romney haven and inlet. a) Ward's map published in 1952 b) Andrew Plater's map drawn in 1998. If we disregard Ward's 'Northern Limen', which is now disproved, his map shows remarkable similarity to that of Plater, based on geological evidence which was not available to Ward 46 years earlier

Old Romney (*see* **37**). While this has yet to receive detailed geological attention, it is as narrow as the northern channel described above, and at present seems a most improbable Rother.

The *Anglo Saxon Chronicle* illustrates the attraction of these sheltered inlets to potential invaders when, in 892, the Marsh suffered a visit from the Vikings:

> The great Danish army . . . were provided with ships [at Boulogne], so that they crossed [the English Channel] in one journey, horses and all, and then came up into the estuary of the *Limene* with 200 [alternative versions say 250 or 350] ships. That estuary is in East Kent, at the east end of that great wood which we call *Andred*. The wood is from east to west 120 miles long, or longer, and 30 miles broad. The river comes out of the Weald. They rowed their ships up the river as far as the Weald, 4 miles from the mouth of the estuary, and there they stormed a fortress. Inside were a few peasants, and it was only half made. Then immediately afterwards Haesten came with 80 ships up the Thames estuary and made himself a fortress at Milton [near Sittingbourne], and the other army made one at Appledore.

This provides a marvellous picture of contemporary geography, emphasising how the Marsh was isolated by the Weald from the rest of Kent and Sussex. Dr Whitelock translated the *Limene* as 'the Lympne estuary', lending considerable weight to the suggestion that the Viking fleet entered the northern *Limen*. But we can now assume that that channel was never of sufficient size to be used by a fleet, and anyway had dried up by the late ninth century. The invaders must surely have used the Romney inlet, and probably the *Wainway*. It only remains very difficult to identify any possible credible location for the half-built fort.

During the Saxon period the marshland cycle of marine advance and retreat reached a stage when, having deposited a good thick layer of silt and clay, the sea left the northern part of the marshland in such a state that it could be occupied all year round. For the first time land was secured that was to remain habitable until today. There is no known relationship between Roman and Saxon landscape. The new settlers occupied a brand new salt-marsh surface, with the result that today's maps of Romney Marsh proper bear the imprint of the salt marsh of 1500-1700 years ago, to which most of the church sites and most of the parish boundaries had been added by *c*.1100.

1 *A lesson in geological sampling. Dr Michael Tooley, on the left with his back to the camera, with students at Bodiam in March 1990. One student is preparing to use a hand auger, another is seated ready to record the samples in great detail. The causeway which carries the road across the Rother valley is on the far side of the field, with Bodiam Castle half hidden in the trees in the background*

2 *A view from a helicopter of the extensive salt marshes at Stiffkey, north Norfolk, showing one main channel and many sinuous creeks. Shallow, water-filled pools are the remains of other, now silted creeks. All this is covered twice daily by high tides, and most of Romney Marsh looked like this at one time or another*

3   Fen carr. Freshwater swamp which persisted
    for several thousand years in the valleys and
    spread out over Walland, and later over part
    of Romney Marsh proper, and now survives
    as peat. A coppiced alder with multiple
    trunks can be seen on the right, a thin
    silvery trunk of a birch tree on the left, and
    tussock sedge at a low level. Trees were
    coppiced to produce firewood, charcoal and
    timber for sea defences

4   An upward succession of blue clay, a dark
    layer of fibrous peat, and a second clay,
    capped by a clay sub-soil churned up by
    ploughing. The peat has only been preserved
    because it was sealed in by the impervious
    layer of clay. Its top is irregular, showing
    that the sea broke over it with some force
    and eroded the surface before depositing the
    upper clay. The handle of the trowel, 6in
    (15cm) long, provides a rough scale

5   A good view of the c.5,000-year-old peat beds on the foreshore near Pett, after a storm had scoured away the beach sand.
    After only a few more tides, the peat was already covered by a slippery veneer of silt. The rectangular cuttings show that
    this peat bed was intensively exploited for fuel, probably in the medieval period, but the peat cutters had to work round a
    log which lay in their way

6   A Roman cremation assemblage of the early second century AD. The cremation urn is at the back, behind two second-
    century Samian dishes and two glass vessels. Some of the bone fragments found in the urn are in the foreground

7 *Scotney Court Quarry, where evidence of salt-working on a buried Roman land surface was first noticed in 1989. A layer of pink briquetage lying on the surface of a buff-coloured clay had been covered by about 3ft (1m) of brown silt mixed with pebbles. This illustrates conditions in which archaeologists, geologists and volunteers often have to work, slipping around on a wet clay surface*

8 *The white walls of Stutfall, the Roman shore fort, stand out slumped low on the hillside below Lympne Castle (at top right). The harbour has not been found, but it must have been somewhere in the foreground of this picture. The Royal Military Canal is hidden in the line of trees in front of the hill, and the channel in the foreground is the Canal Cut of 1878*

9   Looking north-east along Baldwin's Sewer, named after Baldwin Scadeway, tenant of Christ Church Priory, Canterbury. This was a major feature of the planned landscape of c.1150, an efficient straight watercourse running down the centre of the Misleham estate, gathering up water from minor ditches on either side. It remains the main drain of this land now, after 800 years' use

10 Medieval landscape uncovered in advance of gravel extraction. The earliest ditches, in area Lydd 1, incorporated existing winding natural channels, and were dug in the twelfth century. Later, some were straightened. Double ditches flank two medieval tracks which ran along the shingle ridges, heading north-east towards Lydd. Most of the occupation sites have been found beside the tracks, at the sides of the ridges. The quarry is bounded on the south-west and north-east by a medieval embankment known in the sixteenth century as Gorys Wall, but now as Burnthouse Wall

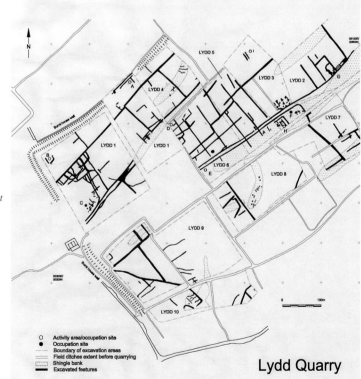

11 St. Clement's, Old Romney
is a small church, serving a
community which was
always small. This isolated
church illustrates several
features typical of most of the
Marsh churches. It stands on
a mound, some 4ft (1.5m)
above the level of the
surrounding fields. It is
surrounded by a ring-ditch,
which runs around outside
the graveyard fence. Note the
sturdy buttress on the south-
west corner of the church
tower, necessitated by
subsidence when the marsh
soils dried out

12 St. Nicholas', New Romney, is an
imposing town church, emphatic evidence
of a thriving and prosperous twelfth-
century community. This photo was
taken in 1981 looking up Church
Approach, then on the line of the twelfth-
century rectangular town grid. Since
then, the local council has diverted the
road, to lessen the dangers of the cross-
roads beside the church. On the left are
the fine early eighteenth-century
Assembly Rooms.

13 *The back, inland, side of the Great Wall near Hawthorn Corner, Midley, where it towers some 8ft (2.5m) above the low ground on the landward side. A slight depression can be seen along the back of the wall, which would have been the back ditch (known as the delph ditch) from which the soil was dug to build up the wall*

14 *Part of the 1258 extension of the Rhee Wall at Old Romney, looking east in 1983. The southern bank can be seen beyond the first three sheep, with two hawthorn trees growing out of it. At this point the road stands on the northern bank, and has evidently been built higher with the addition of road-building materials*

15 *The Newlands estate belonging to All Souls College, Oxford, mapped by Thomas Clerke in 1589. Note the contrast between the pre-1287 landscape of small fields north-east of the green 'sea wall' and the very much larger fields to the south-west of that wall. The north-west boundary of the estate (beneath the coat of arms of the college) is a remarkably straight, artificial, ditch which was dug in c.1500 when the college carried out a joint reclamation with the neighbouring landlord, Christ Church Priory, Canterbury. In 1589 the extreme south-west of the property was still unreclaimed salt marsh at the head of the Wainway. ASC KeS/8*

16 *The site of Broomhill church in 1983, before it was excavated, showing the scatter of building materials in the plough, and the long, narrow mound, then of unknown origin. Later excavation confirmed that the mound was a pile of large building stones brought up by the farmer's plough and thrown aside to be out of the way*

17 *The excavation of the north-west corner of Broomhill church, looking west down the line of the north wall, with the interior on the left. The wall is supported on the outside, to the right, by two buttresses. Note the neatly faced flint on the outside face of the wall, and its rubble interior. This can be compared with the archaeological plan (42)*

18 *A burial in the Broomhill churchyard. One undisturbed grave was found outside the chancel, tidily laid out with the feet resting on fragments of tile and slate*

19 *The gradual decay of Broomhill church recorded in the side of a trench. Some time after the church had been abandoned as a result of depopulation, the sea flooded in and deposited 2ft (60cm) of silt. While the sea was there, the roof fell in, depositing a thick layer of tiles in soft mud. Some ended up banked against the south wall in the foreground. The white line shows that sometime later still, the plaster came off the wall. Above that, the soil has been churned up by modern ploughing. A late-stage sandstone bench-seat can be seen alongside the south wall, and beyond that on the left is one of the octagonal pillars*

20 *The New Gate of New Winchelsea with, to the left, the steep slope of the deep Town Ditch. The name New Gate is somewhat misleading, since it had been built by 1330. This line of defence was abandoned in 1414, because the town has shrunk greatly*

21 The road from Rolvenden across the Rother
    Levels to the Isle of Oxney runs along part
    of the Knelle Dam, and Potman's Heath
    Cottage sits on the dam. On 21 January
    1985 the occupants looked out over the
    road to extensive floods filling the 'wet
    level' to the south. If the house had been
    there between the 1330s and 1630s they
    would have looked out northwards to the
    river Rother

22 Map of Craven Level, at the east end of
    Wittersham Level, made by Thomas Hill
    in 1688. Drawn with north at the bottom
    of the page, this shows the Rother flowing
    down the canalised Craven Channel into
    the tidal Appledore Water through the
    Craven Sluice, which Richard Hudson
    had built earlier in the 1680s. Originally
    the sluice had three outlets, but in 1688
    there were only two. An indent in the
    bank and a wooden structure out of place
    shows that a third had evidently been
    'blown up'. The Craven Sluice finally
    silted up in 1730, and the Rother was
    transferred to the Scots Float Sewer, its
    present course, which is shown at top right.
    The precise size of every field is recorded in
    acres, rods and perches, so that scots could
    be calculated exactly.
    ESRO ACC 2806/1/9/4

23 *The Highknock Channel near Knock, at the east end of the Isle of Oxney. This is the shrunken relic of the* Appledore Water, *down which the Henry VII's warship, the* Regent, *was floated from Reading in 1490*

24 *Flooding of the Rother valley at Bodiam in 1993. Only the upland on either side and the two raised banks of the river remained above the floods, which nearly reached the castle moat*

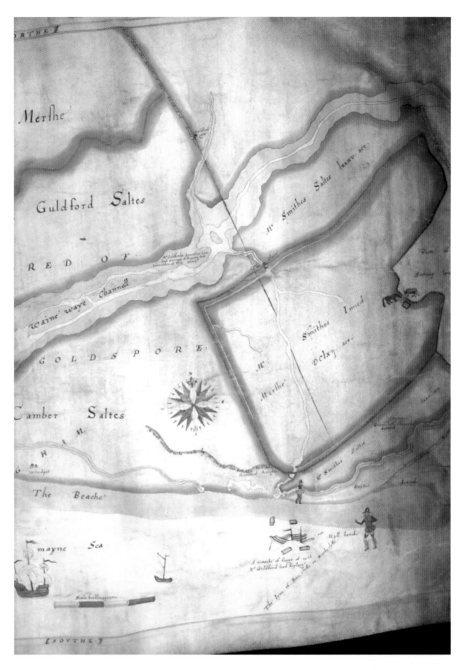

25   *Part of a map of Broomhill and Camber in c.1590, probably made to illustrate a dispute between Sir John Guldeford and Richard Smith over ownership of salt marsh. It shows extensive 'saltes' (salt marshes), Mr Smith's 667 acres of 'inned marsh', and the* Wainway Channel *where (in small writing) 'Mr Guldeford's ancestors have had anchorage of shipping . . .'. On the Camber Saltes was 'a wall intended to be made by Mr Smith but forbidden by Sir John Guldeford'. 'Broomhill church decayed' is marked outside the south-east boundary of Mr Smith's 'inned marsh'. Note the surveyor with his sight lines along the Kent Ditch and on Beachy Head, and the wreck of sugar on the beach.*
ASC KeS/15

26 *The view through the gateway to the central tower of Camber Castle. The lower part of the tower was built in 1512-14, and was heightened when surrounded by the curtain wall and gatehouse in 1539-43. When it was built the castle was very remote, surrounded on three sides by water, hence all supplies, including stone from local quarries and wood from Hornes Wood in Appledore and Knelle in Beckley, had to be brought in by either lighter or wagon. Now it is over a mile (1.6km) from the sea*

27 *Fairfield flooded. This shows what can happen very quickly if the pumps are not working. The hurricane in October 1987 brought down all the power lines, putting the pumps out of order for ten days. The sheep pastured here had to be moved to higher pasture on the other side of the Great Wall. Compare this to the photograph on the front cover*

28 *A hazard of building where peat is near the surface. Hazelden House was built on the side of a wall, part of which can be seen on the right. When the peat beneath the field dried out and partially wasted away, the surface of the field 'sank', while the wall did not. The house therefore tilted. An addition to the left-hand side now appears to prop up the rest of the house*

29 *Blackwall South pumping station in Wittersham Level lifting flood water from the 'wet level' on the left up into the Rother, in February 1990. Installed in 1970, the metal grid covers a pair of Archimedes screws, and the swirling water shows that one screw is working. The fields on both sides of the river are flooded. The sheet piling on the further bank of the river is picked out by the winter sunshine, and the river is within 3ft (1m) of the top of its bank*

30 The Green Wall nearly breached south of Lydd in March 1990, when an onshore gale coincided with a high spring tide. This is looking east, with the sea out of sight on the right, Lydd away to the left, and the Dungeness power stations in the far distance straight ahead. The clefts show that breaches start at the back of banks, rather than by erosion of the front. The fan of rubble at front left was produced when sea water forced its way through rabbit holes, carrying the clay of the wall with it. The Green Wall was breached in the same storm 1.5 miles (2.5km) east of this

31 Defending the Dungeness Power Stations in February 1983. Dungeness A is in the distance, Dungeness B with its circular reactor building is nearer the camera, and the switching station is out of sight on the left. The sea is on the right. All the shingle between the power stations and the sea had been dumped there by lorry, and all was removed in the storms in November 1984. Now the coastline in the foreground has retreated further, and this end of the concrete road, previously used by shingle lorries, has been lost

5 Gaining ground

The twelfth and thirteenth centuries were dominated by rapid and sustained growth of the population of England, and of Western Europe. This created a demand for new land, a pressing need that was to continue until the ravages of the Black Death in 1348-9. Salt marshes were one kind of marginal land which might well be taken in, but only if the climate was favourable. Fortunately, the period from *c*.1100 seems to have been marked by relatively calm weather, at least until the 1230s, without any series of major storms to which the marshes are so vulnerable.

The reaction to this need was different on Romney and Walland Marshes. As we have seen, the documentary evidence of charters, Domesday Book and Domesday Monachorum, combined with the pattern stamped on the landscape by the watercourses, shows that most of Romney Marsh proper had been colonised in the Saxon period. On the other hand, the lack of such evidence argues strongly that Walland was not settled until after 1100. In addition, there is a very clear and significant difference between the pattern of parish boundaries in the two areas.

Since most of Romney Marsh proper was already settled by *c*.1100, that settlement could only become more dense, and two difference kinds of evidence show that this happened. A field-walking study carried out over 655 acres (265ha) found more pottery sherds dating from between 1050 and 1250 than from any other period, which suggests that the population reached an all-time peak at that time. Evidence of former house-sites was found distributed every six acres (2.4ha) — an amazing contrast to the empty landscape of today. Similar evidence came from field-walking carried out on the line of a possible by-pass for Dymchurch. Secondly, a picture of innumerable small fields shows up on aerial photographs, suggesting that the earlier large ones became divided up to meet the needs of a greatly increased number of tenants. Although this subdivision cannot be dated from photographic evidence, the field-walking evidence strongly suggests that it occurred in the twelfth and thirteenth centuries.

Our interest, however, focuses on Walland Marsh and the area south and west of that, most of which was apparently still a vast expanse of salt marsh in *c*.1100. It was a backwater area sheltered from the forces of the open sea by the great shingle bank which still stretched across from Cliff End to Lydd and on towards the inlet at Romney. This area offered great opportunities for expansion, and evidence from a wide variety of sources shows that very rapid, widespread colonisation did indeed take place. The frontiers of the land were pushed forward from every direction (**27**).

We start by looking at the parishes of Walland, as they were in 1878 before being rationalised at the end of the nineteenth century. In contrast to the generally round-shaped parishes of Romney Marsh proper with their churches usually near the centre, those of Walland parishes are long, narrow, straight-sided slices orientated in a north-east/south-

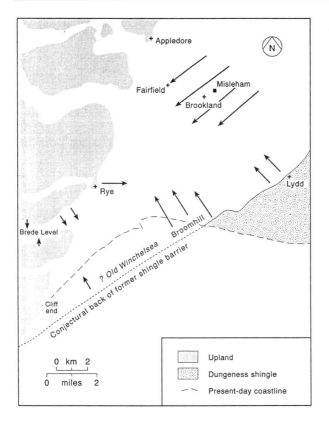

27 *A schematic sketch map showing that in the twelfth and early thirteenth centuries colonists were advancing into Walland and adjacent marshes from just about every direction*

west direction (**28**). This arrangement gave each community a share of the marshland that had relatively good thick soil on top of the peat, as well as a share of the salt-marsh resources further south-west. The latter included peat for fuel, fish and fowl for sustenance, reeds and rushes for the roofs and floors, and possibly salt. Most significantly, several of the parishes (Snargate, Brenzett, Ivychurch, Old Romney and New Romney) are extensions of those in Romney Marsh proper, a strong indication that Walland was colonised by the communities already established on Romney Marsh. Only three churches were founded on Walland itself. Of these, Brookland and Fairfield were relatively late, thirteenth-century foundations (*see* **cover illustration**), and there is doubt about the origin of Midley. Because a place named Midley is mentioned in the Domesday Book, it has always been assumed that the Midley on Walland Marsh was a pre-Conquest foundation. But the entry is strange: it includes both woodland and pig pasture which are not characteristic of marshlands, and indeed were not reported anywhere else on Romney Marsh. In addition the church, now an isolated ruin, stands on a low sandbank which the Soil Survey and geologists recognise as being between two major tidal channels connected to the Romney inlet (*see* **26**). This hardly seems a suitable site on which to establish a pioneering settlement from which to reclaim salt marshes! So altogether there must be considerable doubt about whether Domesday refers to the Midley in Walland Marsh at all.

The landscape of Walland Marsh is also notably different from that of Romney Marsh proper, and there are also great variations in the patterns of the size and shape of the fields

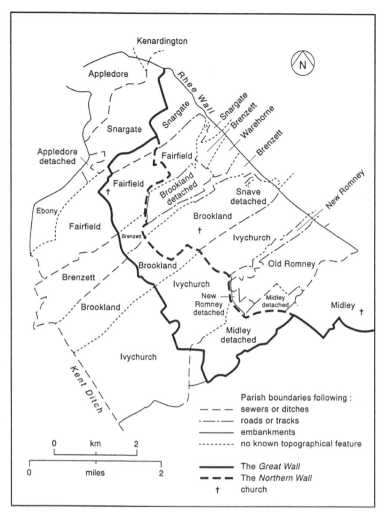

28 The parish boundaries of Walland Marsh — as they were before late nineteenth-century rationalisation. Note the long, narrow, north-east/south-west slices. Five of them were extensions of parishes in Romney Marsh proper, which very strongly suggests that Walland was colonised from Romney Marsh proper. Only three parish churches were founded on Walland Marsh itself

across Walland itself, implying that they were reclaimed at different times and under different economic and physical circumstances (**29**). For the purposes of description here it is divided into three zones. If we assume that the colonisers moved out from Romney Marsh proper, they must have started in the north-east and moved progressively south-westwards, so the zones are numbered 1-3 moving in that direction (**29, inset**). The zones are separated by two embankments, which for simplicity are described here as the *Great Wall* and the *Northern Wall* (**28, 29**). Zones 1 and 2 are described in this chapter, and Zone 3 in chapter 7. Zone 1 has a sub-rectangular pattern of very small fields and numerous roads reaching down from the north-east. This is a 'busy' landscape, which must reflect a dense population. Zone 2 has a much less regular pattern. In Zone 3 the fields are very much larger and, with one notable exception, are irregular in shape, and in that zone there are very few roads. That is a remarkably empty landscape, which strongly suggests that by the time it was reclaimed the economic situation had changed significantly from that which dominated Zone 1.

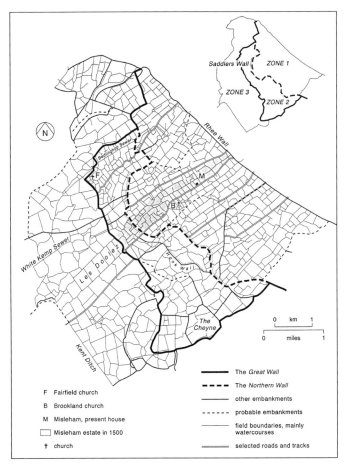

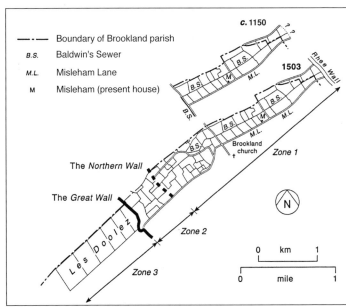

29 *The medieval landscape of Walland Marsh. The ditches and walls are taken mainly from the 1960 1:25000 Ordnance Survey maps — and had altered very little since medieval times. Since then, however, much of this landscape has been ploughed up. Note that the two walls are divisions between very different types of landscape. To the north-east is a pattern of small, sub-rectangular fields. To the south-west of the* Great Wall *they are much larger and irregular in shape*

30 *How Misleham grew, c.1150 – 1500. Two stages in the growth in a south-west direction of the Misleham estate belonging to Christ Church Priory, Canterbury. This estate was exceptional in that its fifteenth-century fields, although very much larger than the earlier ones, were still laid out on a sub-rectangular pattern. Compare it with the adjacent land shown in* 29

The broad outline of the colonisation of Walland can be traced by looking at the documents that have survived for one estate, Misleham, together with its landscape (**30**). The greatest surprise is the elongated shape of the estate. Never more than a third of a mile (550m) wide, it was eventually 3.3 miles (5.4km) long, and it occupied half the parish of Brookland which was split, as it were, down the middle.

Misleham had been given to Christ Church Priory by King Æthelwulf in the ninth century, remarkably early for Walland Marsh. Unlike the Saxon estates on Romney Marsh proper, no pre-Conquest boundaries or landscape features have been identified there, but that is hardly surprising because of the wholesale transformation of that landscape, to small sub-rectangular fields, which was to follow. The earliest phase of the transformation dates from mid-twelfth century when Prior Wibert (*c.*1152-67), who was renowned in Canterbury as an innovator, contracted with a leading tenant Baldwin Scadeway and his sons to hold as much land at Misleham 'as he could enclose against the sea at his own expense'. In 1191 Prior Osburn gave a similar charter to Baldwin's son Simon. Then sometime between 1191 and 1213 Prior Geoffrey gave the 'Men of Misleham' five charters each concerned with an area of 35 acres (14ha), which they were to defend 'against salt and fresh water with walls and waterganges'. Four of these blocks of land have been identified with the 138 acres (55.85ha) which lie on the north-west side of Misleham Lane. From this it is apparent that the main drain, Baldwin's Sewer (which today still bears the name of the twelfth-century tenant), ran down the centre of the estate, collecting water from the minor ditches on either side (**colour plate 9**). The so-called 'walls' which bounded the estate are very minor, scarcely perceptible, banks. Misleham Lane runs along one, and another unnamed lane runs along the bank which forms the south-west boundary (**31**). There is no evidence, from either geology, landscape or documents, that the sea was anywhere near there at that time, so it seems that the function of these so-called 'walls' was simply to mark the boundaries of the estate and the limits of the drainage jurisdiction of the Christ Church tenants.

The pattern of small fields continues as far as the *Northern Wall*, so it is assumed that this land was reclaimed soon after Baldwin's work, under the same pressure of population. Further south-west again, in Zone 2, the landscape is less regular. This cannot easily be explained but may be due to difficulties in draining it: the peat is very near the surface. Then we come to the *Great Wall*, a massive embankment which shows that something very dramatic happened. There, for everyone to see on the ground, is clear evidence that the sea had broken in and that action, probably very urgent action, had to be taken to keep it out. This, however, must have happened after the period of calm weather had ended, and the story is continued in the next chapter (*see* page 77).

No similar documentation has survived from which to reconstruct the development of any of the other parallel estates in Walland, although most of them also belonged to big ecclesiastical landlords. The other half of Brookland belonged to St Augustine's Abbey, Canterbury; Ivychurch to the Archbishop; Fairfield and Old Romney were other properties of Christ Church; and Brenzett was the property of an unknown lay landlord. Similar landscapes and parish boundaries suggest that their history must have been very similar to that of Misleham. They too were long and narrow in shape and had similar patterns of watercourses, field systems and roads which lead down from the direction of

31 Misleham Lane, a straight track which was an important feature of the twelfth-century planned landscape. On the north-west side of this lane some of the field boundaries still survive and, remarkably, it is possible to establish the names of the tenants who held those fields in 1503

Romney Marsh proper. They too are crossed by the two defensive embankments. This strongly suggests that several parallel estates were pushing south-west, moving their frontiers out into a hitherto uncolonised salt marsh more or less simultaneously — and that their progress was eventually halted by a widespread influx of the sea.

The general outline of this remarkable exercise in 'countryside planning' of the twelfth century remains stamped on the landscape today. The watercourses slant north-east/south-west across the map. A number of roads, mostly little lanes, still do the same and close scrutiny of the six-inch Ordnance Survey map of 1878 shows that there used to be other green lanes which are now lost from the landscape. We can imagine all these being used as the access and drove roads for the men of Romney Marsh proper as they developed and exploited the rich potential of Walland.

Here, then, is evidence of twelfth- and early thirteenth-century landscape-planning on a very grand scale. Surveying and digging all the straight watercourses must have made tremendous demands on manpower, and would probably only have been possible at a time of dense population. On the other hand, once the straight watercourses had been dug, they had several advantages over the alternative, which were sinuous former salt-marsh creeks. They provided the shortest, quickest and most efficient means of conveying water from one point to another, and minimised the problems of erosion of banks on the bends.

At much the same time as colonization was taking place in Misleham and the adjacent estates, the same thing was happening west of Lydd where, as far as we know, the salt marsh had not been occupied since around AD200. There, although post-medieval ploughing has destroyed the surface evidence, the systematic investigation which is taking place in advance of gravel extraction at Lydd Quarry is providing an exceptional opportunity for archaeologists to assess the lower levels of the very extensive medieval landscape still preserved beneath the disturbed topsoil (**colour plate 10**). Excavations are producing a rich supply of artefacts and structures, which are supplying information about how the people were living (something that was not available at Misleham). Once the topsoil has been stripped off, a very complex pattern of ditches is revealed, which can be dated by the remains of coarse pottery thrown into them. The story that is emerging shows that in the first half of the twelfth century winding salt-marsh creeks were cleared out and used as boundaries of small, irregular-shaped fields. No occupied sites have been found dating from that time, so it is assumed that during that early phase the farmers lived in Lydd and walked out to the fields, day by day.

In the next phase, in the later twelfth and early thirteenth century, they started to live on their land. At that time the ditches were straightened and small simple dwellings were established beside two tracks, spaced out about one every 6 acres (2.4ha) — a density remarkably similar to that on Romney Marsh proper in the same period. Only the foundations have survived the ploughing, but the houses were probably simple timber-framed structures with roofs thatched with straw or reeds. Cattle, sheep or goats and pigs were kept, cereals were grown, and quantities of shells show that the peasant farmers' diet included oysters and cockles. The pottery consisted predominantly of coarse-ware cooking pots, a few bowls and crude jugs. A very small quantity of fine ware had come from Scarborough and France, and querns (hand mills for grinding corn) were made of lava imported from Germany. Progressive quarrying and archaeological investigation are expected to continue for several years to come, so we can expect that more detail will be added to this picture of medieval life on the Marsh.

At Broomhill, some 3 or 4 miles (5-6km) further south-west, colonization also began at a similar time. Here no landscape evidence has survived, since the area has either been overrun by the sea or completely lost because the coastline has receded. But details have survived in written documents in the archives of Robertsbridge Abbey. That provides more information about the names of the people involved, if less about how they lived. Family groups started reclaiming the marsh in the twelfth century. Among these entrepreneurs the best-documented is the Doudeman family, who were also known as the 'Men of Broomhill'. They must have been of considerable local importance, since their name survived for at least two centuries in *Dudemanswick*, a place (now lost) in Hope All Saints near New Romney. The gavelkind system of inheritance, whereby a tenant's land was divided equally between all his sons, ensured that the family worked as a closely-knit group especially when dealing with ownership and exploitation of their land. By the early thirteenth century their property had become divided between eleven grandsons of the original Doudeman and, to take an example, when the abbeys of Battle and Robertsbridge

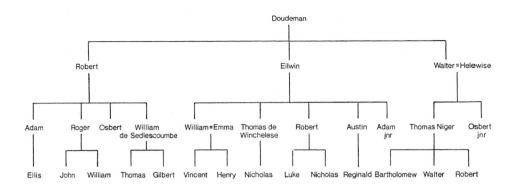

32 Four generations of the Doudeman family, the 'Men of Broomhill', in the twelfth and early thirteenth centuries. The intra-family co-operation required by the gavelkind system of inheritance meant surviving charters have provided sufficient detail for Dr Mark Gardiner to construct this family tree

started buying up the land soon after 1200, Adam the son of Eilwin had to give his brothers and nephews other land in exchange for their shares before he could complete a sale. These records also provide genealogical interest, for it has been possible to construct a Doudeman family tree from a time several centuries before parish records were kept, which provide the source-material for present-day genealogists (**32**).

A very large area of Broomhill was reclaimed in this early period, between the sea and shingle on the south, near which there was a church, and a wide channel described as the *'Water of Cheyne'* on the north. Just one of Doudeman's pieces of marsh amounted to 600 acres (245ha). Later on, in 1222, Battle and Robertsbridge abbeys combined in a venture to enclose a further 1,400 acres (570ha). The two continued their reclamation confidently until about 1240. But after that they must have had doubts about the security of their marshland because in 1243 they made an agreement with a condition attached that payment of rents for a certain enclosed marsh would cease *if that land was overwhelmed by the sea*. After that date, no records of further reclamation have survived.

Several individuals who were involved in reclamation at Broomhill were involved in similar work in the Brede valley. Although surviving records are relatively limited, a similar progression can be detected there. Advances were made in the twelfth century, but after the early thirteenth silence fell. Further south, probably just behind the shingle barrier, reclamation of the salt marshes also went ahead towards the end of the twelfth century and continued until the 1230s. For example, in *c.*1197 marshes between *Old Winchelsea* and Cliff End (the name still given to the east end of the Fairlight cliffs) were granted to Robertsbridge Abbey. In *c.*1210 the abbey received another grant, of marsh 'in the moor below Rye'. Reclamation must have still been proceeding confidently in the marshes east of the *Water of Rye* in the summer of 1234, when the monks of Robertsbridge were allowed to reclaim as much land as they reasonably could. Although at that date it was envisaged that further reclamation would take place within 10 years, in fact there are no records that this ever happened.

The overall picture that emerges is one of a similar sequence of events in widely-spaced areas and from a wide range of sources. Contemporary documents show that from the mid-twelfth century onwards large-scale reclamation was taking place at Misleham, at Broomhill, in the marshes to the south and east of Rye, and in the Brede valley. Landscape evidence combined with the parish boundaries indicates that what was happening at Misleham was far from isolated, and that advances were made on a broad front, moving south-westwards from Romney Marsh proper. Archaeological excavations at Lydd Quarry, an area for which no documents survive, have shown the same sequence. In all these areas widespread and large-scale advances took place into previously unoccupied salt marshes, much of which belonged to monastic houses.

The question therefore arises as to what this colonisation of salt marshes (a process also described as 'reclamation' or 'inning') involved. As we have seen in the example of Misleham, tenancies were granted on condition that 'walls and waterganges' were provided and maintained. This simple phrase describes the two structures that are fundamental both to initial reclamation and to longer-term maintenance of all marshlands, in other words, to human survival there. The banks kept the sea and/or fresh water out, and the watercourses were essential for draining away the fresh water. So, at its simplest, the primary reclamation described in this chapter involved enclosing a specific area with an earth bank, and at the same time making arrangements for joining up the watercourses and letting the water out through the bank by means of a sluice, otherwise known as a gutt.

In this period of high population and settled climatic conditions, ports also flourished. The site of *Old Winchelsea* was somewhere out in what is now Rye Bay, probably not far outside the present mouth of the Rother. Like New Romney, this town must have stood on the relatively high and well-drained ground of the early shingle barrier. But while the port of Romney was deserted by the sea and the townsite did at least survive, *Old Winchelsea* was undermined and washed away in the thirteenth century. So any idea of its position or that of its harbour can only be, at best, conjectural.

Its early history is very sketchy. The whole of Sussex from Hastings eastward was included in the vast Saxon manor of *Rameslie*, which was granted by King Canute *c.*1017 to the Abbey of Fécamp in Normandy. Domesday Book recorded that this manor included an unnamed new town, in which there were 64 burgesses, but whether this was *Old Winchelsea* or Rye is still being debated. Neither of them is mentioned by name. The manor also included 100 salt-works, an exceptionally high, if nominal figure. This simply indicates a large area of unreclaimed salt marsh, where salt-extraction was a very important industry.

Somewhat more is known of the twelfth century. Both *Old Winchelsea* and Rye are mentioned in the Pipe Rolls, lists of ports and the taxation levied on their merchants, in 1131 and 1164-5. Their first surviving charter dates from 1191, but confirms liberties granted to them back in the reign of Henry II (1154-89). By 1190 they had joined the association of the Cinque Ports as the 'Two Ancient Towns', although in 1191 their shipping was still very inferior to their head port, Hastings. Their period of prosperity really seems to have begun around 1200, for in 1204 *Old Winchelsea* featured as the third in the list of ports on the south and east coasts, only London and Southampton surpassing it. Moreover, *Old Winchelsea*, whose merchants paid £62, was a considerably more important centre than Rye, which only contributed £10. In the 1220s both towns flourished as centres of shipbuilding, and in 1235 they possessed a striking display of naval strength. *Old Winchelsea* had nine ships, the largest of them being 160 tons, and Rye had four including one of 240 tons and another of 170. Between 1237 and 1243 there were royal dockyards and storehouses in both towns. Everything points to the conclusion that while both towns were active through most of the twelfth century, their greatest period of prosperity began about 1200. In addition, Rye was very closely related to *Old Winchelsea*, but at that time was of secondary importance.

Romney was a significant town and port by mid-eleventh century, but which Romney was this? This is a question that has been widely debated. There are two settlements. The hamlet of Old Romney lies 2 miles (3km) west of the small town of New Romney. In addition, the sea is now over a mile (2km) east of New Romney, and there are no signs on the ground of the once flourishing port. The obvious inference is that Old Romney, with its isolated little church dedicated to St Clement (a dedication which was common in the early eleventh century) was the original port (**colour plate 11**). It might be argued that this silted up, causing the focus of activity to shift seawards, to the site of New Romney. However, the combined evidence shows that that is not what happened.

All the early documents refer simply to Romney, and the prefixes 'Old' and 'New' are relatively new, much later than the settlements they describe, and so are misleading. The name 'Old' Romney only dates from the thirteenth century, while the prefix 'New' did not appear until the fifteenth. We have already seen documentary evidence of a very early settlement on the site of New Romney, when an oratory dedicated to St Martin stood near the mouth of that *Limen* when King Æthelbert of Kent granted his fishery to the minster at Lyminge in 741. This must be assumed to be the precursor of the large church of St Martin which stood in medieval times beside the Ashford Road in New Romney (*see* page 61). All the available evidence indicates that Romney, which we now know as New Romney, rose from those early beginnings. It stood, unlike Old Romney, on the firm basis of a shingle bank. By the eleventh century it had become a town and port of considerable strategic and commercial importance. The town plan and the architecture of the remaining church show that it went from strength to strength and was a very prosperous settlement in the twelfth and early thirteenth centuries. The streets in the centre of town are laid out on a striking square plan, while those on either side, to the north-east and south-west, appear to be on a second rectangular grid. In addition, the pattern of parallel north-east orientated streets is continued in the lanes and landscape out in the country on the north-west side of the town, showing that it was once a much larger settlement than it is today (**33**).

St Nicholas is a very impressive building, standing testimony to a thriving community (**colour plate 12**). The nave and two side aisles date from early in the twelfth century: four pairs of solid Norman columns, alternately octagonal and rounded, survive at the west end. The two lowest stages of the tower were built in the 1150s or '60s, and it was completed in the 1180s. There is, however, an unfortunate dearth of documentary evidence. Domesday Book has no entry dealing specifically with Romney, although entries dealing with other manors do confirm that it was a large and thriving town. It had

33 *An oblique aerial photograph of the planned but shrunken town of New Romney, taken in 1953. We are looking down the line of the High Street and other parallel streets. The rectangular pattern of cross-streets is less obvious. The triple roofs of St Nicholas' church can be seen on the left, and the big open space to the right of the High Street is the site of St Martin's. Note also several parallel lanes without housing to the right (north-west) of the town, evidence that the town once covered a much larger area*

at least 156 burgesses, of whom 85 were tenants of the Archbishop's manor of Aldington.

In contrast, a field-walking exercise undertaken in 1990 in an attempt to find out whether Old Romney had also once been a much larger settlement, found no evidence that there had ever been a major settlement there. It is concluded that Old Romney must have always remained a minor, up-river, settlement.

Economically, the twelfth and thirteenth centuries were a time of prosperity. It was also a time when the increasing population resulted in land hunger, and landless people were enticed on to the Marsh. Until about the 1230s the climate also favoured expansion in the marshes. Recent archaeological work on Romney Marsh proper and near Lydd has provided evidence of a dense population. To the south, on Walland and other nearby marshes, very extensive colonisation of salt marshes was possible. A plentiful supply of new land was matched by a large workforce, and the maritime frontier was pushed back radically and rapidly, mirroring what was taking place at the same time elsewhere. For example, great dyking activity is recorded from Holland, and advances were made in the English Fens. Climatic stability also favoured the coastal harbours. Romney, *Old Winchelsea* and Rye, all presumably blessed with sheltered and relatively stable havens, flourished as commercial centres and in all likelihood some of the profits made there were reinvested in reclamation schemes to secure more new land. But all this depended on that climatic stability, and we have already seen certain ominous signs. The great defensive wall at Misleham shows that at some point the reclamation process went into reverse. A record from Broomhill, where the landlords realised that it might not be possible to retain some new land, shows there was a reason for caution. And although the lack of any surviving grants of marsh for reclamation after *c.*1240 does not in itself prove that reclamation ceased, the same pattern emerging from Broomhill, the Brede valley and near Rye is likely to be more than a coincidence.

6 Thirteenth-century crises

The time from the 1230s to 1290 was one of climatic extremes. The monastic chroniclers, our principal source of information, described exceptionally heavy and prolonged rains, deep and lengthy frosts, thunderstorms, gales and whirlwinds, as well as strange cosmic happenings. There were also, as far as we can tell, three spells when there were repeated and violent storms — in 1236, 1250-2, and 1287-8. Overall, this was one of the most tempestuous 60 years on record.

Coastal marshlands are particularly vulnerable to storms, especially when several occur in quick succession, and during this period there were numerous reports of flooding and disaster from the coastal districts of England, Wales and the Low Countries. Storms disrupt coastal defences. A quick visit to a shingle beach in a gale should be enough to convince any reader that the shingle is mobile. High winds generate big waves that move vast quantities of shingle, greatly accelerating the process of longshore drift. Also, when an onshore gale coincides with a high spring tide, sea water will percolate through the shingle and may cause the bank to collapse and a gap, or breach, will occur allowing the water to flow inland. The breach may or may not be repaired naturally, according to whether a sufficient supply of new shingle arrives from further along the beach. As well as this, stormy weather promotes higher tides, which flow further inland up the rivers. And, when an intense low pressure system passes up the English Channel, more water than usual is drawn eastwards, building up and causing a *surge*. A similar surge in the North Sea also tends to raise sea level in our area. Although the chroniclers did not specifically mention such things as surges, medieval records have to be interpreted with these physical processes in mind.

At this time Romney Marsh, a high-risk area, suffered great changes. In 1230 it was still protected on the south and east by the ancient shingle barriers. But by 1290 the southern barrier had disintegrated and the town of *Old Winchelsea*, which must have stood on that barrier, had been lost. The loss of the protective barrier allowed the sea to flow inland, and thousands of acres of marshland, much of which had been reclaimed in the previous two centuries, were converted back to salt marsh. The tides also flowed many miles up the rivers. The eastern barrier weakened, so that in 1288 the first phase of the Dymchurch Wall had to be built. The port of Romney became severely silted, and the massive earthwork known as the Rhee 'Wall', actually a watercourse, was constructed in an attempt to wash away that silt. Also, in response to the stresses caused by the storms, the nationally-important *Laws and Customs of Romney Marsh* were defined and written down. In this chapter, we follow first the progress of destruction and inundation in the south, and then turn north to Romney and the Rhee before finally discussing the *Laws and Customs*.

The southern barrier, together with the town of *Old Winchelsea* and its port, were swept away in those 50 years. That piece of coastline has gone, and so the story of the cataclysmic changes which took place there have to be reconstructed on the basis of written records. The first of the great floods occurred in 1236. Exceptionally heavy rain in January, February and March flooded roads, bridges and causeways, and the situation was made worse when the influx of a spring tide in March held back the outflow of the rivers. Then in November a great inundation caused much damage and loss of life. Three senior officials were sent out from the Archbishop's manor of Aldington for three days to Romney, *Old Winchelsea* and Appledore, to 'see to the preservation of . . . the Marsh against the inundation by the sea'. By 1244 at the latest, *Old Winchelsea* was in need of protection against the sea, for the burgesses were allowed to raise a levy of 2 shillings on every ship entering the port with 80 or more tuns of wine, in aid of constructing a 'quay' 'for the defence and improvement of their town'. The problems were on-going, as that permission was repeated in the following year. In 1247, for political reasons, Henry III took *Old Winchelsea* and Rye back into English control after more than 200 years in French hands (*see* page 22). In 1249 problems with sea-defence were evidently increasing, since the town was given a large grant, 130 marks (£86), by the Crown 'on condition that they are diligent in repairing and preserving the town against the sea'. Rye was given 70 marks (£46) at the same time. The town was thus in considerable trouble even before the horrendous storm of 1 October 1250, which was described by Matthew Paris, a travelling monk who acted as a roving reporter. Even after making allowance for the journalistic exaggeration for which he was renowned, that storm was clearly catastrophic. It coincided with a spring tide and apparently a Channel surge, which would be a very difficult combination at any time. He wrote that

> the troubled sea crossed its usual bounds, flowing twice without ebbing, and gave forth such a horrible roaring and crashing that it resounded in places remote from it. At *(Old) Winchelsea*, besides salt-cotes and the retreats of fishermen, as well as places of refuge and mills, more than 300 buildings were destroyed in the same district by the violence of the sea.

While the salt-workings and tide mills would have been out on the salt marshes and major creeks, and accustomed to occasional over-washing, the loss of houses must have been exceptional. With defences no doubt badly weakened, the sea overflowed again the following winter. In 1251 the Crown sent two senior officials to 'provide and order how the town of *(Old) Winchelsea* can be saved and defended from the sea . . . to the protection and security of the adjacent country' — which included the marshes of *Old Winchelsea*, Rye, Pett Level and the Brede valley. The freemen and owners of land all across the Marsh, from *Old Winchelsea* to Hythe, were included in the discussions. In other words, the sea-floods and raised water table affected the whole marshland, but at this stage the southern flank came off worst.

Already in serious trouble, *Old Winchelsea* suffered a second onslaught, on 15 January 1252. Matthew Paris gave an eye-witness account:

A raging east wind and an angry south-westerly wind occasioned much damage. . . . If we are silent about other injuries and damage we will introduce an account of what we experienced. At the harbour of *(Old) Winchelsea*, . . . the waves of the sea, as if indignant and furious at being driven back the day before, covered places adjacent to the shores and drowned many men.

The following year, in the wake of that great storm, the sea once again over-flowed its banks. Land was salted and crops failed.

The pace of change on the coast is greatly accelerated by storms, and the sea evidently made great advances in 1250 and 1252. Very little, if any, of the lost land would have been recovered. In 1258 at the latest, sea water was running up to Appledore, and was being diverted down the Rhee to Romney (*see* page 84). Three years later, when the barons of *Old Winchelsea*, Rye and Hastings were summoned to attend the king at Lydd, they had to cross 'the arm of the sea', which shows that there was already a wide inlet somewhere near Rye.

In the 1250s and '60s *Old Winchelsea* lost more ground. In 1262, for example, the 'imminent peril of the waves and violence of the sea' constantly threatened the town. Streets were described as ending abruptly, at 'the sea on the south'. In 1271 a large part of the church fell into the sea after the defences beside it were carried away by the tempests. Erosion continued relentlessly until in November 1280, when the old town was already 'for the most part submerged by the sea', the king's steward, Ralph of Sandwich, was sent to obtain land on which to rebuild the town on its present hilltop site. In 1283 Stephen de Pencestre, Lord Warden of the Cinque Ports, and other senior officials began laying out the streets and plots of the new town. The grid pattern of unusually wide streets that they created remains the basis of the present town.

Old Winchelsea was, in the words of Matthew Paris, 'a very necessary town to England and especially to London'. It was the principal port receiving wine from France, and also provided a large proportion of the fish consumed in the capital. It is all the more remarkable that throughout the upheaval of relocation it continued to trade as the principal port on the Sussex coast.

The progressive disintegration of the southern barrier must have laid the marshes behind it, which would naturally have been lower-lying, increasingly exposed to the prevailing south-west winds and waves. As the sea advanced, defences would have been erected and almost undoubtedly some would have been abandoned. But what remains for all to see is the *Great Wall*, which was mentioned briefly in the previous chapter as a very significant feature of the landscape crossing the Misleham estate (*see* **30**). This exceptionally massive embankment zig-zags across the Marsh from west to east and then turns south to Broomhill (**34, colour plate 13**). Part of it was known as the *Great Wall of Appledore*, presumably because it protected the land of the Christ Church manor of Appledore that included detached outlying land at Fairfield and Misleham. It was being maintained as early as 1258, when tenants were making payments for its upkeep. So it must have been built progressively higher and thicker over a period of 30 years or more before the rapid succession of three great storms in 1287-8. That progressive preparation must explain why it was able to resist the onslaught of the culminating storm on

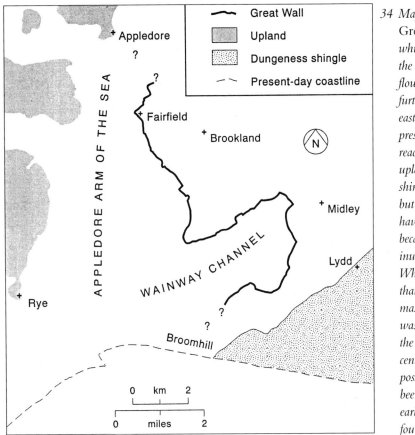

34 *Map of the Great Wall, which prevented the sea from flowing any further north or east. The wall presumably reached from the upland to the shingle barrier, but both ends have been lost because of later inundations. While it is clear that this massive rampart was built up in the thirteenth century, it could possibly have been based on earlier foundations*

4 February 1288, which was described by the chronicler Gervase of Canterbury:

> the sea rose to such an extent . . . in the marsh of Romney and all the adjacent places that all the banks were broken down and almost all the lands covered from the *Great Wall of Appledore* . . . towards the south and west as far as *(Old) Winchelsea.*

What he did not say explicitly was that without it, the sea might have overrun the whole marsh. As well as being a very substantial landmark, it is also a major boundary. To the south and west the land is higher, because of the layers of sediments brought in by the sea during the storms. The soils differ from one side to the other, being younger on the south-west. And there is also a sharp distinction between the pattern of older, small, rectangular fields to the north-east and that of large irregular fields to the south-west (*see* **29**).

It is worth considering a short length of this wall in detail, because it illustrates how the thirteenth-century inhabitants dealt with some of problems which confronted them. Irregularities in the line of the wall south of Brookland highlight some places where the sea managed to break through (**35**). At the point where the Fairfield road leaves the main A259 south of Brookland, a great southward loop follows the repair of a breach. The tidal

35 Landscape evidence of some breaches in the Great Wall *near the Woolpack Inn, south of Brookland*

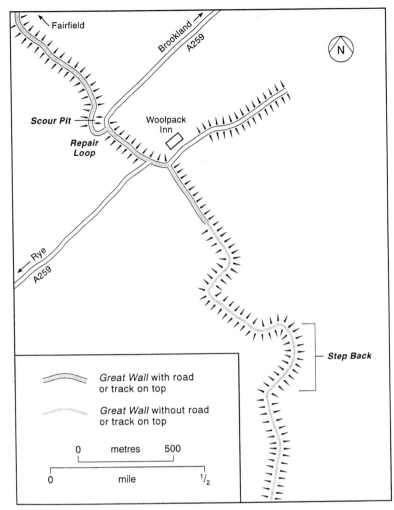

water rushed in and out through the narrow breach and created a scour pit, which is now represented by a rush-filled depression. It was not practicable to build a new length of wall straight across this deep pit, so a horseshoe-shaped repair wall was constructed to avoid it. The substance of the repair wall has since been removed, so that the road is at marsh level at this point, but the horseshoe remains imprinted on the landscape. The wall evidently also gave way a short distance to the south-east, and there it was necessary to rebuild a short length of it further back. There is no reason to think that the breaches in sea banks which took place then were materially different from those which occur today. Now, they usually take place at high tide in winter storms, often after dark, and the inrush of water is sudden, noisy and very frightening. Emergency repairs have to be undertaken under very difficult and daunting conditions. So it is not perhaps surprising to find that the *Great Wall* was backed up by a second line of banks, the *Northern Wall* (*see* **28, 29**). This was altogether a less massive structure, but no less useful. Some parts of it exhibit similar

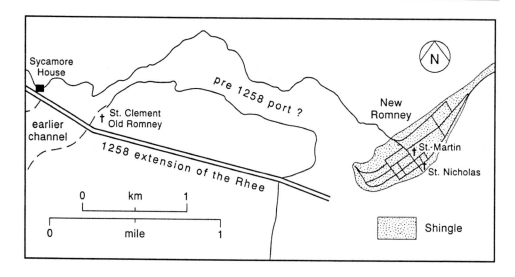

36 A conjectural map of the haven of Romney, based on the Soil Survey map. It shows two stages in the life of the haven. Some time before 1258, the tidal channel was open from New Romney westwards to Old Romney, and ships could have anchored in it, sheltering from storms in the English Channel. At that stage the Rhee ended west of Old Romney. By 1258, however, the haven had been blocked by obstacles, and the Rhee was then extended down to a point within half a mile (800m) of New Romney

changes in land-levels and in soils from one side to the other, which show that it did on occasions serve to prevent more extensive flooding.

At the same time as the sea was making devastating advances in the south, on the east coast it was retreating from the port of Romney, also with disastrous consequences. The town of New Romney relied for its prosperity on its haven, where passengers could embark, goods could be loaded, and shipping could shelter, all out of the reach of the rough water and storms in the English Channel. Interpretation of the Soil Survey map strongly suggests that this port was based on a channel which extended west towards Old Romney and then originally continued south-west as the *Wainway* (**36**). The tidal channel would probably have been narrow, and so the shipping would probably have been anchored prow to stern for a considerable distance along it, as pictured at Rye by Prowez in the sixteenth century (*see* **65**). As long as sufficient tidal water was flowing in and out to prevent the inlet silting up, the town prospered. But the earliest documentary evidence available shows that by 1258 at the latest it was already very seriously silted, and this silting must have been going on for a considerable time before that. That must have been critical for the town.

The story of the decline of the port is intimately bound up with the Rhee, an artificial watercourse which was cut from Appledore to Romney to bring water all the way across the Marsh to flush away the accumulating silt. An extraordinary achievement, it was eventually over 7 miles (11km) long and came within half a mile (800m) of St Nicholas'

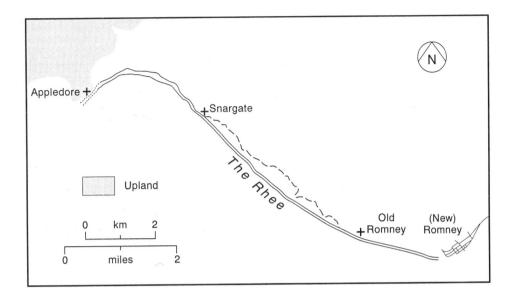

37 A map of the Rhee. In spite of being named a 'wall', the Rhee was an artificial watercourse running between two walls. It was built in at least three stages to convey water to flush out the harbour of Romney: Stage 1, from Appledore to Snargate. Stage 2, from Snargate to Old Romney. Stage 3, from Old Romney to New Romney. Only the last can be dated, at 1258. This map also shows, as a dotted line, the low bank and winding channel which seem to be associated with the Rhee system

church. The Rhee is one of the largest and most obvious features of the whole Marsh, but also one of the most difficult to understand. Landscape evidence suggests that it was built in several stages, and the only document available describes the last of these, built in 1258. We have to consider with it a low bank which the Soil Survey mapped running from Snargate to Old Romney on the north side of the Rhee, and beside that a minor, very sinuous channel (**37**).

At present it is only possible to suggest a hypothetical sequence of very determined attempts that were made to prevent the inlet and the port from becoming silted up. The following is a model of what may have happened. When the port was flourishing, the inlet extended inland to Old Romney and then turned south-west. Although the river known much later as the Rother had probably reached the sea there in the past, it must be emphasised that the important, powerful force was the tides. It was the twice-daily ebb of the tides which kept the inlet open. However, the more silted that became, the faster the silting proceeded.

The earliest man-made feature near the Rhee was the minor bank on the north side of the small watercourse. This was probably constructed in Saxon times as the defining boundary between the reclamations on Romney Marsh proper and the extensive salt marshes which then stretched away to the south-west. Significantly, this bank stops at Snargate, because the area north-west of there, including the Appledore Dowels, remained unreclaimed until well after Domesday. The channel beside the bank was originally dug to provide the soil for the bank. Later on the sea broke in, enlarged the eastern end of the channel and greatly magnified its curves.

When the Romney inlet began to silt up (the natural fate in due course of all the Marsh inlets) the release of the water from the minor channel into the inlet was controlled by a sluice that stood near Sycamore House, some 700 yards west of Old Romney church. For a time this water helped to wash away the silt, but when this proved insufficient, a much more elaborate scheme was adopted. The first phase of the Rhee was dug between two banks to convey fresh water of the Rother from Appledore to Snargate and empty it into the top of the northern channel. This did not help for long, so the Rhee was then extended a further 3.2 miles (5km), to empty the water from Appledore into the Romney inlet at Sycamore House, providing a greater flow than was previously available. However, the storms of the 1250s blocked the inlet from Old Romney to New Romney. The king intervened, having been informed that the existence of the port was threatened. The report of his advisor, Nicholas de Hadlow, dated 28 June 1258, is the earliest surviving written record of the Rhee:

> the king has understood that the port of *Romenal* is perishing to the detriment of the town, unless the course of the *river of Newenden*, upon which the said port was founded can be brought back to the said port, and he now hears . . . that the river cannot be brought back, or the port saved, unless the obstructions in the old course be removed, and a new course made . . . near the old course.

It proved impossible to remove the obstructions, which may well have included the remains of shipping shattered in the storms of 1250 and 1252. So the Rhee was extended again, in a third phase (the 'new course'), from its sluice near Sycamore House, 'down to the said port' (**38, colour plate 14**). The whole system operated as a gigantic lock, or indraught, bringing a supply of water right across the Marsh. The flow was controlled by three sluices. The first, at Appledore, took in sea water which was flowing up from *(Old) Winchelsea* and retained it, together with some river water when the tide went down. The second was at Snargate, and the third controlled the outfall into the port, and kept out the tides at that end.

Thus by 1258, in spite of large-scale efforts to prevent this happening, Romney had lost its valuable sheltered inlet. Its fortunes declined because from then on it had to rely on much smaller port facilities nearer the open sea. The Rhee apparently continued to keep that open until the sluices were removed early in the fifteenth century. This remarkable structure now stands proud above the marshes on either side, mainly due to more recent wastage of the peat underlying the adjacent marshland, especially on the north side between Appledore and Snargate. It may be remembered that the Victorian engineer Elliott suggested that the Rhee was a Roman structure. However, it cut across a late-Roman channel near Old Romney (noted on page 44), and must therefore be later than that. It also cuts straight across the twelfth-century extensions of the Romney Marsh parishes, and so must be later than those. As shown here, it was constructed to keep the port of Romney open, and it seems most probable that it dates entirely from the thirteenth century.

38 *An aerial view of the last phase of the Rhee Wall, looking east over Old Romney, with the church on the left. The two parallel walls which enclosed this artificial watercourse stretch away towards New Romney. The present-day road runs along the left, northern, bank, while the southern bank is alternately a upstanding bank or a slope where the bank itself has been ploughed out. On the far side of Old Romney the structure clearly cuts across field boundaries, which shows that it was a very late addition to that landscape. Note the concentration of houses lined up along the Rhee, because the silted watercourse provides the highest and driest land for miles around*

Further north, the shingle barrier guarding the Dymchurch coast seems to have stood up to the earlier storms of this century. Not until February 1288 is there any mention of problems there. But then, just after the last of the three great storms, an urgent order was issued at a meeting at Snargate. A new wall was to be built at *Holewest* (Dymchurch). It was to be 40ft (12m) wide at the base, narrowing to 20ft (6m) at the top, and 12ft (3.7m) high. Work was to start on it in the first week in February, after one month it was to be

6ft (1.8m) high and it was to be finished by Easter, 28 March. The speed required clearly shows that this was emergency work. Although, unfortunately, we do not know how long it was, its height shows that this was another massive structure, which was presumably needed to plug a gap which had opened up when some of the shingle moved away towards Hythe. It seems, therefore, to have been the first phase of building the great Dymchurch Wall.

That Romney Marsh proper was spared inundation before this was presumably due to the *Laws and Customs*, a legal system which provided for mutual cooperation to provide for the security of the marshland. The principle was that all landholders (which invariably meant the tenants, at least from the sixteenth century onwards) should contribute to sea defence and land drainage in proportion to the acreage they held. The special nature of marshland means that arrangements for water control are essential, and in general the operations in the early days cannot have been very different from those of today, except that we have the benefit of power-driven pumps. From the beginning, the earliest Saxon landowners surrounded their estates with low banks which were used for water control and as property boundaries. Within each estate minor, private ditches were connected to main waterways known as common sewers. The movement of water along the watercourses was, and still is, controlled by stop-boards. The sewers lead to sluices which control the outflow of fresh water at low tide and keep the sea out of the marsh at high tide. As watercourses quickly become blocked by vegetation and silt, sluices decay and banks are degraded, the system requires constant maintenance. From the beginning, therefore, there must have been agreements between landowners and tenants and between neighbours to ensure that this was carried out. The earliest surviving documents describing this are from the time of Henry I (1100-35). The success of the twelfth-century expansion at Misleham and in a much wider area, shows that a well-managed system must have evolved by the mid-twelfth century. We must assume that certain officials were in charge, administering the system, although no documents have survived to describe them. We only know that by 1250 there was already an organisation of 24 officials, known as jurats, elected by the people of the Marsh to enforce contributions for the maintenance of walls and watercourses for the benefit of all. Until as late as 1288 their responsibilities included maintenance of the *Great Wall of Appledore*.

While that system and administration worked well in the period of calm weather before 1230, it was not adequate to cope with the climatic challenges of mid- and late-thirteenth century. The walls were not strong enough to face the storms, the cost of their repair increased sharply, and disputes broke out in protest against unusually high charges and the threatened breakdown of the system. This led to royal intervention. In the wake of the storm of 1250, existing arrangements needed to be clarified and authority reinforced. In 1252 Henry III was, in the memorable words of Dugdale 'so tender . . . for the preservation and security of this famous and fruitful marsh' that he granted a charter to the jurats. He confirmed their ancient powers to levy contributions from every landholder in proportion to their acreage, and also commanded the Sheriff of Kent not to 'meddle' with the fines they imposed for non-payment. Henceforth complaints were to be made direct to the king. Five years later the marshlanders were resisting further payments, as a result of which 'the banks and waterganges being not repaired, the sea and other waters overflowed this marsh'. The problems clearly included disposal of fresh water as well as maintenance of the sea banks, and the king sent his chief political and judicial officer, Henry of Bath, to sort matters out. At a meeting with the people of the Marsh and representatives of Kent at Romney on the 14 September 1258, he issued his famous Ordinances. On that occasion both the length of all the sea banks and the total area of marshland were measured, and each landholder was allotted responsibility for a specified length of wall, in proportion to the acreage he held.

In November 1287 the sea banks were once again broken by the violence of the sea, and Edward I sent John de Lovetot and others to investigate, as a result of which the authority and integrity of the bailiff was reinforced. In addition, the boundaries of Romney Marsh were redefined. It had been illogical for some time that the responsibilities of Romney Marsh should still reach south to the *Great Wall*, since the area beyond the Rhee had been effectively severed from Romney Marsh proper by that watercourse. So arrangements were made for a separate bailiff and jurats to act in that district (later named Walland Marsh) initially under the supervision of the officials of Romney Marsh. Similar arrangements were made for the marshes of Oxney and Lydd. There were, of course, later disputes which were settled by further enquiries, and a system of payment by scots evolved (*see* page 100), but the basic arrangements were retained, and confirmed repeatedly in charters by later kings. The responsibility and authority remained with the lords (the landowners), the bailiff and the jurats.

Thus the substance and most of the details of the *Laws and Customs of Romney Marsh* were defined and encoded by higher, external authority in response to the stresses caused by the extreme storminess of the thirteenth century. This system was, and still is, of fundamental importance to the survival of not only Romney Marsh but also all other marshlands in the country. Innumerable medieval commissions ordered other English marshlands, many of which were far away, to regulate their affairs 'according to the law and custom of Romney Marsh'. Locally, the system evidently operated so well that when the Land Drainage Act of Henry VIII in 1531 established Commissions of Sewers for all other marshlands, the Lords, Bailiff and Jurats of Romney Marsh retained their own autonomous organisation.

The storms of the thirteenth century tipped a very delicate balance. The stable protection which the shingle barriers had hitherto given the marshes in the south and at Dymchurch was ended for ever, and from thenceforward artificial sea defences were needed on a much larger scale than ever before. In the wider economic context, the national population was still increasing and urgently needed additional land and food supplies. But Romney Marsh could no longer provide these. On the contrary, the reduction of productive land there probably started in the 1230s, and by the 1250s the inhabitants were beating a very serious retreat.

7 The aftermath

The weather of the thirteenth century left Walland Marsh storm-shocked. Sea defences must have been exhausted and financial resources depleted. Then, before the marshland had recovered, the national economy ceased to expand and a downturn set in. The causes and timing of this are still being debated, but it seems that the very unfavourable weather between 1315 and 1322 which led to failed harvests, famine, and disease in sheep and cattle, only reinforced economic and social problems which already existed. Soon afterwards, agriculture was further hit by falling prices and high taxation. In 1348-9 the Black Death reduced the population to perhaps 40% of its former size, and thereafter recurring epidemics of the same bubonic plague served to keep numbers down. Thus, by the time it was physically possible to reclaim lost land, the demand for it had ceased. By the time Walland Marsh was eventually reclaimed in the fifteenth and sixteenth centuries it was used as pasture, and seems to have been providing raw material for the woollen industry in the Weald. Against this background, in this chapter we look at the ultimate recovery of Walland, the surprising survival of Broomhill church when most of Walland was tidal and, briefly because very little is known about it, the history of New Winchelsea. Finally, we look at the day-to-day operations needed to maintain the Dymchurch Wall, a work of medieval engineering without parallel anywhere else in England.

We look first at Walland. After 1288 most of the area south and west of the *Great Wall* must have been tidal. The sea deposited a layer of sediments, up to 10ft (3m) thick, outside the wall. Away from it, a new pattern of salt-marsh creeks was established and silting continued there. There is no evidence by which to date this deposition, but it seems very likely that most of the deposits near the wall would have arrived during the great storms, when the tides would have been at an exceptionally high level. Then, although the sea continued to make occasional incursions over the next two centuries, particularly between 1377 and 1400 in the 'old', low-lying land in the Appledore-Snargate-Fairfield triangle, and threatened to do so in part of Broomhill in the 1360s and '70s, the marshland pendulum had swung once again and from the fourteenth century onwards the sea was in retreat. Analysis of a sequence of manorial accounts suggests that this was already happening at Fairfield early in the fourteenth century (**39**).

The new land-surface which the sea left behind it was higher and drier than most of the rest of the Marsh, but there is no evidence to show that it was reclaimed quickly. Rather the opposite. The first evidence for that comes early in the fifteenth century when in 1416 a wall round *Ketemarsh*, 500 acres outside the *Great Wall* at Fairfield, was measured (**40**). The landscape shows, moreover, that by the time this 'new' land was reclaimed the economic climate had changed. Gone were the carefully-planned, small sub-rectangular fields of expansionist days, serving a dense population. Instead, the new generation of colonists

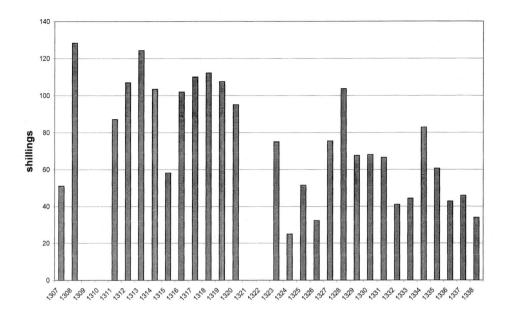

39 This graph, which is based on an almost complete sequence of accounts for Fairfield, shows a definite decrease in expenditure by that manor on sea defence and land drainage between 1307- 39. Sea defence was much more costly than ditching, and the graph therefore supports the suggestion that the sea may already have been retreating during this period. Note that the accounting year ran from Michaelmas (29 September) to Michaelmas

reverted to the practice of adopting the former salt-marsh creeks as their drainage channels, and produced much larger, often irregular-shaped fields suitable for use as extensive pasture. The striking difference between the old, pre-1287 landscape inside the *Great Wall* and the new colonisation outside it is still apparent on the Ordnance Survey maps of today. It can be seen on figure **29** and, even better, on a map made in 1589 of the Newlands estate belonging to All Souls College (**colour plate 15**). Eventually, by 1600, walls had been built and the sea shut out from most of Walland Marsh (**40**). In 1478 and 1497 the Guldeford family bought up over 4,000 acres (1,600ha) of salt marsh from Robertsbridge Abbey. Arriving on the scene at a time when the sea was naturally retreating, they walled in large areas, so that by 1600 Guldeford Marsh was also reclaimed. This left only two fast-diminishing tidal inlets, the *Appledore Water* (otherwise known as the *Appledore Arm of the Sea*) running from the south coast up to Appledore, and the *Wainway Channel* (or *Creek*), a crescent-shaped inlet running from Rye in the direction of Lydd.

Broomhill, lying on the south side of the *Wainway*, had a surprisingly different history from the rest of Walland Marsh. A ruined church is shown there on most of the maps of the 1590s as well as on some modern Ordnance Survey maps (*see* caption to **colour plate 25**). As that site is one of very few historic landmarks near the south coast of the Marsh, it holds an important key to understanding the evolution of that particularly mobile coastline. We have already seen that there was a church at Broomhill in the early thirteenth

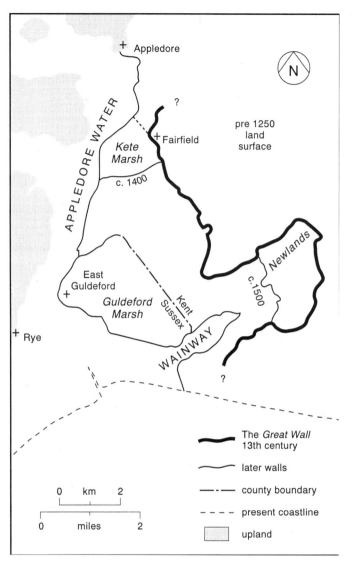

40 *Post-flood reclamation of Walland Marsh and Guldeford Marsh, 1400-1600*

century. But by the early fourteenth century a large area of Broomhill had been lost to the sea. Robertsbridge Abbey had sustained 'great loss of land' in the marshes of Winchelsea, Rye and Broomhill. Battle Abbey also suffered losses there: in the thirteenth century it had been receiving rent for certain 'new land' in Broomhill, but in the early fourteenth century the beadle noted laconically that it had 'sunk beneath the sea'. Three centuries later Camden added a touch of drama to the story. Presumably relying on local folk-history, he stated that in the reign of Edward I (1272-1307) 'the sea, driven forward by the violence of the winds, overflowed this tract, and . . . threw down Broomhill', forcing the inhabitants to flee to Lydd.

A great deal depends on whether this was indeed the site of the *c*.1200 church. Or, since one medieval reference to *Old Broomhill* suggested there could have been two churches in succession, could this have been a replacement for an earlier church which had been lost? In an attempt to resolve at least some of the questions concerned with its history, the site was excavated in five short seasons from 1985 to 1989. The surrounding geology was explored at the same time, as were documentary records that might refer to changes in the coastline.

In 1983 the site was marked by a wide scatter of fragments of building stones, red tiles, slate, and large, mortared flint cobbles in a ploughed field, and by a long narrow grassy mound (**colour plate 16**). This indicated that the remains of a building did indeed survive beneath the soil. In addition, the absence of a mound of suitable size and a surrounding ring-ditch, characteristics of nearly all the marsh churches (*see* **cover illustration** and **colour plates 11, 27**), suggested that whole site had been buried by a thick layer of sediments brought in by the sea, which is even now less than a quarter of a mile (350m) away.

Initially two trenches were dug across the narrow mound, which was found to be formed mainly of lumps of building stone, thrown on to a heap after they had been brought up by the farmer's plough. Short lengths of walls were also exposed. A resistivity survey was then used, very successfully, to locate the other walls (**41**). This method of remote sensing showed up not only the outline of a small church with a chancel, but also

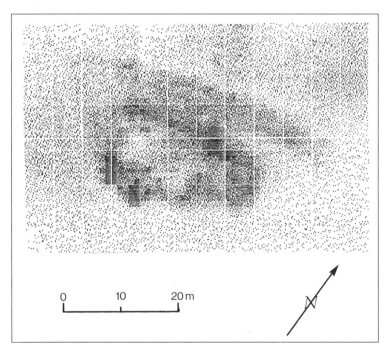

0   10   20 m

41 This dot-density plan of Broomhill church was produced by a resistivity survey, a remote sensing method undertaken by Dr Andrew Woodcock and Dr Mark Gardiner. It proved most successful in detecting the walls of the buried building, showing the narrow chancel and the south porch. It also showed up a structure running parallel to the north wall, which was proved by excavation to be a churchyard wall built of flint

another structure to the north, which turned out to be a collapsed churchyard wall built of large flint cobbles. The excavations showed that the church had been built on soil above a buried shingle ridge. A quantity of pottery which included domestic jugs found on a burnt surface outside the west end, a midden including shells and fish bones under the churchyard wall, and a deposit of grain and chaff beneath the chancel, all showed that the site had been used for other, unknown, activities before church-building began.

The church itself had undergone four phases of building and alteration, which was in itself very surprising in view of its remote and rural situation, though the first two phases were probably short-lived. In the first, deep foundations were dug, but were probably abandoned. The second was represented by a crude sandstone wall, with footings that ran under the floor of the third phase and were incorporated into a buttress of the third phase. This phase was represented by the north wall and part of the west wall (**42**, **colour plate 17**). The north wall was almost a metre thick, with an outer facing of rounded flint pebbles and occasional rounded sandstone blocks. The core was filled with rubble of the same materials. Finally, the south wall was moved outwards, leaving parts of it forming an arcade and creating a narrow aisle, and a southern porch was added. The new wall was built of neatly faced courses of flint cobbles, the doorways were decorated with well-carved mouldings, and the base of the aisle piers were neat octagonal columns (**43, 44**). This was altogether of a much higher standard than the earlier phases. The inside of the new wall was faced with plaster, and a graffito of a medieval ship had survived on plaster that was still very firmly attached to the wall (**45**). Outside the chancel wall the ground was very much disturbed, indicating multiple burials, but one undisturbed grave was found (**colour plate 18**).

The sequence of events as the church was abandoned and fell into disrepair can be traced in a section along the side of one of the trenches (**colour plate 19**). A thin layer of dirt on the floor showed that the building was abandoned before the sea flooded in. Above that was 2ft (60cm) of marine sediment, in the middle of which was a thick layer of red tiles and the 'ghost' of a rotted timber roof beam, showing that the roof had fallen in all at once while the church was flooded. Some pieces of glazed windows were found directly on the floor, and others were embedded in the soft sediments, indicating that some windows had been blown in before the sea flooded in, and some while it was still under water. Higher up in the marine sediment a thin white line showed that at least some of the plaster had later come off the walls, also while the site was still flooded. Finally, as was only to be expected in an area which offered no building stone except flint, most of the valuable stone had been removed from the building. However, the robbers left parts of the two lowest courses, which suggests that they may have approached across salt marshes, between high tides, when those two courses were already buried by sediment. Less of the flint was taken, presumably because there was no local shortage of that.

Thus the sequence of construction and subsequent deterioration of the church building was explained by excavation, but the problem of dating its origin remains. The pottery from below the church was critical, but unfortunately it was not possible to date that closely enough to say whether it was early thirteenth- or early fourteenth-century. In addition, no coarse-grained sand or pebbles were found which would have been indicative of a great storm. So the church site seems to have escaped the effects of the storms, and

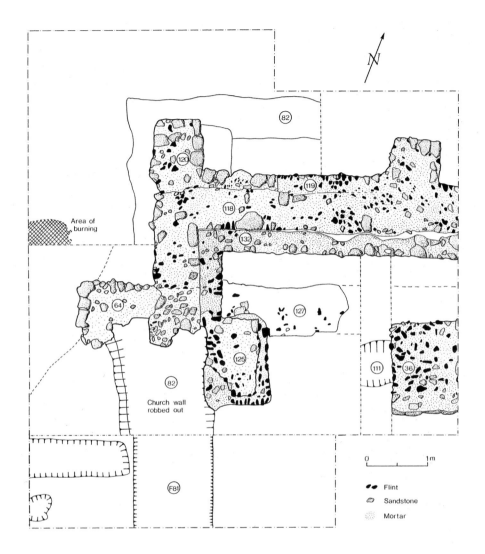

42 Plan of excavated trench D, at the south-west corner of Broomhill church. 111 is a ditch which pre-dated the church building. Traces of a second-phase wall (127) were found beneath the third-phase floor and had been incorporated into 64, a buttress. 118 is the core and 119 the outer facing of the north wall, built in the third phase. A later addition was a low bench (132) found around the inside of the north, west and south walls, to provide rudimentary seating. See also **colour plate 17**

43 *Moulded stonework at Broomhill church surrounded by the collapsed roof tiles. This sophisticated stonework marked the edge of the doorway leading to the south porch, and belongs to the fourth, and last, phase of the building. It is attributed on stylistic grounds to the fifteenth century*

44 *An octagonal pillar base at Broomhill Church, also part of the fourth and last phase of the building. It was surrounded later by a circle of irregular, water-worn blocks of sandstone obtained from a beach. The scale rod is 1m long*

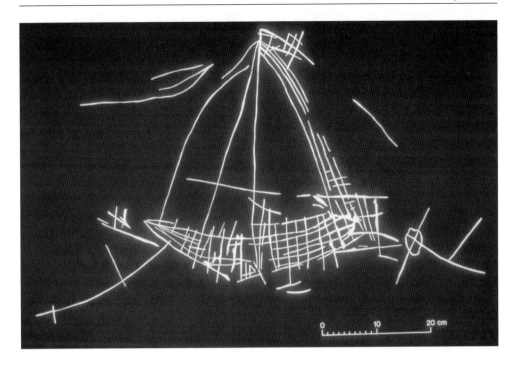

45 Graffito of a medieval ship etched into the plaster on the inside of the south wall of Broomhill church. The plaster had survived there for over 500 years, and all attempts to remove it failed

the question whether the church pre- or post-dated the late thirteenth century remains open. Thus neither the archaeological nor the environmental evidence answers the question. However, to coastal geologists relying on the known pattern of northward migration of this coastline (described on page 115), it seems quite likely that this was a replacement for a building which stood further south and was indeed lost in the thirteenth century. But this too is inconclusive. The later history of the building is somewhat clearer. The finely carved doorways of the fourth phase probably date from the first half of the fifteenth century. Then, towards the end of that century the church went out of use because, owing to depopulation, it was no longer needed.

The fact that it was possible to occupy the church site for so long is in itself surprising. Throughout the time it was occupied, that area must have been protected by a mass of shingle over half a mile away to the south. Indeed, inquiries made in 1365 and 1374 show that the defence of both Broomhill and Lydd depended on an *ancient wall* which lay not on the south but somewhere away to the west and north, bounding what was later known as the *Wainway Channel*. But by around 1500 the southern shingle had thinned out and the sea broke through, converting the area round the church to salt marsh. In *c.*1590 it seems that although some of the valuable building stone had already been removed, the ruin was still visible above ground, for at that date the early cartographers mapped it as 'the ruins of Broomhill church' and Thomas Knight, a jurat of Lydd, referred to it in an inquiry as 'an old piece of a church'. It had yet to be buried completely (*see* **colour plate 25**).

46 The entrance to one of the numerous medieval wine vaults which are a feature of New Winchelsea today

On the other side of Rye Bay, the new town of Winchelsea was founded on its hilltop site in 1280. A rectangular street plan was quickly laid out, with two new churches, markets, and 802 plots (79 of which were down near the harbour), and by 1292 a considerable proportion of the town had been built. A harbour was established on the River Brede at the foot of the northern cliff. The steep track which led down to it from the Strand Gate survives today as one of the entrances to the town. Initially the harbour was evidently excellent, for in 1325 Winchelsea was described as a port where 'on account of its size, several vessels can land at once'. Its first 30 or 40 years were a time of great prosperity. For instance within eight months in 1306/7, 737,000 gallons of wine were imported from south-west France. Sloping doors leading down to the vaulted medieval wine cellars beneath many of the houses bear witness to Winchelsea's principal trade (**46**).

The respite from the problems caused by the sea was, however, short. As early as 1336 the port was said to be nearly filled up with sand and shingle, and the town was given permission to levy dues on every ship entering it, and all goods and merchandise brought to or from the town by land or sea, in order to fund removal of the obstructions and construction of a breakwater. During the Hundred Years' War the ports paid a high penalty for being easily accessible by sea. New Winchelsea was sacked and burnt several times by the French. The most devastating raid was in 1360, when a large force took the town and killed the inhabitants. By then it was also suffering from the effects of the Black Death. In 1384 it was described as 'once well inhabited . . . but now so desolate and almost destroyed' that is was impossible to establish the ownership of vacant plots and tenements.

47 *An aerial view of New Winchelsea, a New Town laid out in the 1280s. A rectangular street pattern, and plots, were laid out covering the whole of the hill-top which is the area with trees. With the aid of a magnifying glass the Strand Gate can be seen at centre left, the Pipewell Gate at the near right corner of the town, and the so-called New Gate is hidden in the trees way out in the country at the far end of town (**colour plate 20**). Initially, most of the town was occupied but, following the Black Death (1348-9) and being sacked several times by the French, almost half the plots were empty by 1366. In 1414 the size of the town was much reduced and a new wall was partially built not far outside the present housing. Some of the original parallel streets can be seen, extending out into the country beyond the present built-up area. The harbour was close below the densely wooded cliff in the foreground*

Refugees from Winchelsea, rich and poor alike, were living semi-permanently in Battle. The size of the town became much reduced, with buildings concentrated in an area not much larger than the present built-up area, and in 1414 a new wall was planned, and partly built, well inside the original limits (**47**). In 1400, problems of silting in the harbour were evidently caused by the mariners dumping ballast in the channel. Between 1419 and 1442 large-scale engineering works took place further up the Brede valley, apparently in an attempt to provide a controlled outflow of water to scour silt out of the harbour (*see* page 105). It appears, however, that Winchelsea continued to be the principal commercial centre in the locality until early in the Tudor period. When the sea finally abandoned its harbour in the second decade of the sixteenth century, Rye took over and prospered in Winchelsea's place. The unusually wide streets of today follow the rectangular grid laid out in the thirteenth century, but the New Gate and grassed-over earthworks to the south of the present houses show how the town has contracted (**colour plate 20**).

In contrast to the advance and retreat of the sea in the south in this period, Romney Marsh proper must have been successfully defended against the sea between 1288 to 1592. In 1288, as we have already seen, a wall was hurriedly thrown up to plug a gap in the shingle barrier near Dymchurch. No records have survived to show what happened between then and the sixteenth century, and when the documentary curtain rises again, the Dymchurch Wall was in place. We can only assume that it had been built up, length by length, as the former shingle barrier gradually moved away northwards, towards Hythe. The earliest surviving accounts show that it was in existence in the 1530s. The best contemporary map, made by Poker in 1617, shows that it was three and a half miles long, almost as long as it is today (**48**). At that stage it was known by various local names, as well as by the overall name of Dymchurch Wall.

It was a remarkable structure, which was sustained by a sophisticated system of maintenance which must have developed, like the wall, over a long time. It was a great rampart of clay dug from the marsh, which was 'armed and fenced against the wash and rage of the sea'. The 'arming and fencing' consisted of a woven lattice-work of thorn bushes and timber work. Faggots (bundles) of thorn as large as men could carry were laid close together in courses and stamped down onto the clay. They were secured by 3-5ft (90-150cm) oak stakes known as 'needles', which had a hole near the top described as an 'eye'. First, half the length of the needles was driven down through the faggots into the clay of the wall. Then long flexible rods ('edders') were woven round the projecting tops of the needles, and short wooden 'keys' were driven through the eyes. Finally, the needles were driven down as close as possible to the clay without breaking the keys.

Maintenance of the wall was a large-scale industry. Repairs to one length or another went on continuously, summer and winter, year in, year out. The work went on non-stop during daylight hours in the winter, and from 6am to 6pm in the summer, whenever the tides allowed, and was very labour-intensive. It is worth considering a document that has survived from *c*.1620 in some detail because, uniquely, it shows how the work was carried out, and gives a flavour of the day-to-day life on the wall. It must also give an indication of how other walls were maintained, for which little or no documentation has survived, for instance the thirteenth-century *Great Wall*, and the Kent Wall in the sixteenth century. The Dymchurch Wall itself was maintained in this way for several hundred years. Not

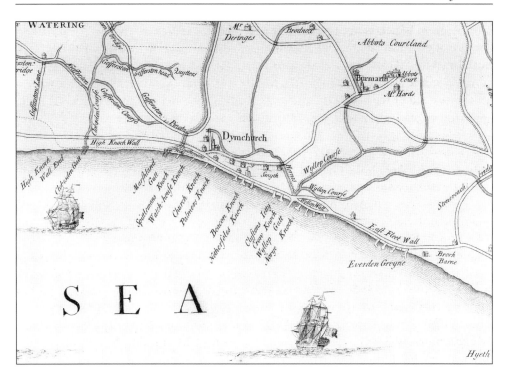

48 The Dymchurch Wall shown on Matthew Poker's map of Romney Marsh made in 1617, with north to the right. This is a faithful copy, made by James Cole in 1735. The wall was already nearly as long as it is now. Note High Knock Wall, Spittleman's Wall, Willop Wall and East Fleet Wall, all local names for different parts of the wall; three outfalls of fresh water through the wall, Clobsden Gutt, Marshland Gutt and Willop Gutt; and 17 'knocks' (groynes), which were filled with rock. Also shown are the sewers, named 'courses'. CKS S/Rm P8A

until the 1820s was any rock used on the seaward slope.

In preparation for repairs, the old timber work was pulled away, any material worth re-using was stored, and the surface of the clay rampart was re-dug, levelled and beaten flat with implements with heavy heads known as 'beetles'. For a month or two in high summer the clay was brought up from appointed fields on carts, which were traditionally 5ft (1.5m) long, 3ft (0.9m) wide and 14in (35cm) deep, each pulled by a horse led by a boy. In 1622 around 200 carts were in action, making two trips a day in a continuous procession. While half were being loaded and going up to the wall, the other half were being unloaded and the clay was being spread out, stamped down and the cart set to rights before making the return journey. Trouble-shooters known as 'goadmen', equipped with a goad (a long stick sharpened to a spike) stood at every corner, to guide the horses and ensure that they did not run over the boys or run out of control down the slope of the wall. If a cart-wheel or a harness broke and brought the procession to a halt, the boys traditionally shouted 'A coye, a coye, a coye', to attract help from the goadmen. Repairs to the lattice-work of thorn bushes and timber often went on all year round.

In addition, the Wall was defended by large groynes known as 'knocks', seventeen of which are shown on Poker's map. From time to time these needed to be repaired or replaced. Their purpose was to hold the remaining shingle in place, in order to break some of the force of the waves before they reached the wall. They consisted of two parallel rows of piles 4ft (1.2m) apart, from the top of the wall down to the sea. The piles varied from 8ft (2.4m) to 14ft (3.3m) in length. The space between the two rows was filled with rocks, some of which weighed as much as a tonne, under which a *carpet* of bushes, brushwood and timber about 1ft (30cm) thick was laid to prevent the rocks sinking into the sand. Near the middle of the wall, where the erosive power of the sea was greatest, a line of shorter piles was added on either side of each groyne, with more rocks filling the space between them, to reinforce the structure and prevent it from being lifted out of the ground by high tides.

An 'engine' known as a 'ram' was used to drive the piles. This was an iron structure 18ft (5.5m) high and weighing 8 hundredweight (440kg), which supported a great wheel with a main rope running round it. It was operated, of course, by manpower and needed 28-30 men. The operation was directed by the tenor man, who pulled the main rope. Attached to that were 24 'ringing' ropes, each pulled by one man. This brought the ram down on the pile, which was bound fast to the middle post of the frame and was kept steady by 'levermen'. Each knock contained 500-600 piles, and if the beach consisted of soft sand it might be possible to drive 60 piles in a day, but if it was stony, only 20. The terminology used to describe this operation of the ram was, interestingly, very similar to that used in bell-ringing.

The weather must have frequently made communication with a large workforce difficult, and there were no factory-style sirens, so at the end of the day the expenditor or his deputy held up his hat on a goad. At the sight of that the boys shouted out 'Harry, Harry, Harry' in memory of Henry of Bath who had drawn up the *Laws and Customs* of the Marsh in the thirteenth century. This was the signal to collect the day's pay and leave for home.

Maintenance of the wall involved very great expense and a large workforce. On 29 July 1622, 203 carts and the same number of 'fillers' were employed to cart clay to the wall. This work went on for 36 days in July and August, costing £395 2s 6d. 'Wallers', who arranged the lattice-work of bushes and timber, worked that year from July to March (often, in other years, they worked all year round). In July an average of 40 'wallers' worked 21 days. By November, always a time of year when the sea made special demands, the number had risen to an average of 80 men working 24 days in the month. Walling that year cost £364 9s 6d. A third major item of expenditure was £445 10s 1½d, paid for buying, preparing and carrying thorn bushes to the wall. The total cost of maintaining the wall that year was £2,391 16s 8½d.

All this reflects and illustrates the detailed operation of the *Laws and Customs* in the early seventeenth century. Romney Marsh was among the most valuable agricultural land in Kent, and without the wall, the sea would have flowed in over it. The very considerable cost of its maintenance was divided between all the landowners (or tenants), as decreed by Henry of Bath. The central pivot of the organisation was the annual meeting (general lathe) of the Lords, Bailiff and Jurats that took place on the Thursday in Whitsun week.

That meeting elected a substantial local landowner as the expenditor, in effect the chief executive, for the year, although in practice individuals often held office for several years in succession, and sometimes went on to become bailiff.

In 1622 a scot of $\frac{1}{2}$d per acre (generally known as a half-scot) raised £48 12s 2$\frac{3}{4}$d. Payment of the scots was spread out over the year, as and when the expenditor needed the money. On the Sunday two weeks before payment was due, scots were 'proclaimed' in five churches spaced out round the Marsh, New Romney, Burmarsh, Newchurch, Ivychurch and Snargate, and in Hythe market on the corresponding Saturday. The owners or tenants brought or sent their scot money to the clerk of the Level at New Hall in Dymchurch on the relevant Monday or Tuesday. On the Wednesday, known as pay day, the clerk passed the money over to the expenditor, who then paid all outstanding bills due, for example, to the suppliers and carriers of the materials. On the same Wednesday the clerk also presented the bailiff with a 'bill of wanes', a list of those owners and tenants who had not paid their scots. The bailiff then tried to secure a double scot from the defaulters. If unsuccessful, he would distrain (appropriate) their cattle, keep them in the common pound for three days and finally sell them if the double scot was still unpaid.

To sum up, during or after its thirteenth-century inroads, the sea deposited a valuable thickness of new sediment on part of Walland and adjacent southern marshes. When it retreated, the land which had been lost in the thirteenth century became some of the highest and driest in the Marsh. For economic reasons, however, it was not speedily reclaimed. When this did eventually take place in the fifteenth and sixteenth centuries, the population had declined to a fraction of its former size, economic need had altered, and the newly reclaimed land was set out as pasture. For the same reason, the older landscape, the small intensely-farmed fields of Romney Marsh and the northern part of Walland, also became grassed over. Main sewers were retained, but many minor ditches were abandoned and gradually filled up with vegetation. This was the origin of the 'traditional' marsh sheep pasture, a carpet of grass covering a fossil medieval landscape, and it remained undisturbed until 1939, since which much of it has been ploughed up.

Lambarde and others have painted a bleak picture of life on the Marsh in the sixteenth century and later, with a very sparse population severely weakened by malaria, known locally as the 'marsh ague'. But it seems that this dismal impression may have been exaggerated. After all, in July 1622 there were at least 250, and in November over 80 able-bodied men capable of 12 hours strenuous manual labour, day in, day out, on the Dymchurch Wall.

8 'Drowned lands': the valleys

The long broad valleys of the Rother, Tillingham and Brede extend westwards from the Marsh, dissecting the Wealden upland (**49**). In addition, the Rother had the very unusual choice of two courses. It could flow either north of the Isle of Oxney, in a course that became known as the *Appledore Channel*, or south of Oxney through Wittersham Level. Because the alluvial soils of the valley floors are much more fertile than the dry acidic sands and intractable clays of the uplands on either side, the land in the valleys (known as levels) was always highly valued. But their drainage was extremely difficult and for much of historic time the levels were more or less under water (**50**).

There are three main causes of drainage problems, which together are formidable. The rivers drain a large catchment in the eastern High Weald of Kent and Sussex, where steep slopes and impermeable soils mean that surface run-off is swift. The valleys are very low-lying, which means that the river water can only flow away to sea during the lower part of the tidal cycle. And, thirdly, until the sea retreated in the eighteenth century it continued to deposit silt in the seaward end of the channels. Three quarters of the annual rainfall occurs in the six months between November and April, so that until pumps were installed in the 1960s, freshwater floods used to occur in winter at the same time as the sea was most likely to flood in up the rivers. In summer, on the other hand, the flow of the rivers was so little that it was frequently insufficient to scour away the silt deposited in the channels and sluices at the mouths of the valleys. With the rivers bringing down fresh water to one end of the valleys and the sea blocking the outlets at the other, extensive flooding was inevitable.

Then there was the human factor. Different groups had different interests in the valleys and their rivers. On the one hand, the landowners aimed to drain the levels as well and as fast as possible. On the other hand, the rivers were important as highways for transporting heavy and bulky commodities such as firewood and timber out of the Weald, and navigational interests required a certain depth of water in the river channels all the time. A number of small ports or docks grew up along the valleys, for example at Float Farm (Udimore) and at Brede Bridge on the river Brede, and at Appledore, Reading, Smallhythe, Maytham, *Knelle Dam* (Beckley), Newenden and Bodiam on the Rother (**51, 52**). Yet a third group became involved in the periods when the ports of New Winchelsea and, later on, Rye were silting up and their livelihood was threatened. The flow of the tides up and, especially, down the river channels was vital for removing the silt from their harbours. Inning of marshes upstream was said by the portsmen (not in every case correctly) to be reducing the tidal influx and there were often strong objections to what was happening upstream. In short, the aims of the landowners (and each of those had his own particular interests at heart), of navigation and of the ports were often irreconcilable.

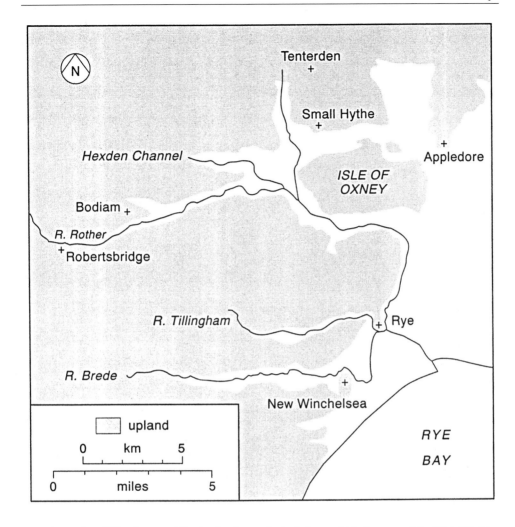

49 *The Rother, Tillingham and Brede, the three principal rivers which flow out of the High Weald of Kent and Sussex and cross part of the Marsh on their way to the sea. The Rother has a choice of two valleys, north or south of the Isle of Oxney – see also* **52**

The history of the valleys provides an excellent illustration of all the problems and conflicting interests involved in marshland drainage.

We have already seen that part, at least, of the Brede valley was reclaimed under the favourable circumstances of the late twelfth and early thirteenth centuries. But those conditions changed drastically before the end of the thirteenth century. When the Rye Bay barrier finally broke down in 1287-8, there was little to stop the tides flowing inland. Around that time the *Damme*, a 1000yd (1km) long bank was thrown up across the valley, with a sluice operated by pulleys to control the outflow of fresh water (**51**). This may have been intended to restrict the flow of the tides, and/or to retain water which was then released at low tide to clear silt accumulating in the new harbour of Winchelsea near the

*50 Flooding in the Rother Levels in November 1960, when the valleys were universally flooded. This aerial photograph was taken looking west up the Hexden valley, one of the main tributaries of the Rother (see **49**). Rolvenden Layne is off to the right of the picture, and Newenden further away off to the left. The banks of the main channel can just be seen above the floods. Note the traces of small square, probably medieval, fields which can just be picked out on the unflooded ground in the centre of the foreground.* Photograph by Skyways Photos

mouth of the river. It was also used as a causeway across the level and the tolls, which amounted to as much as £5 per year in the 1360s, would have contributed towards its maintenance. Though now ploughed out, this embankment was still a prominent feature of the landscape in 1960. In the fourteenth century Wealden firewood was loaded at a dock near Float Farm, later to be shipped to London and the Continent (the name float means a dock, so that has an early origin). The *Damme* probably succeeded in limiting the extent of sea flooding, but that had the knock-on effect of limiting the ebb through the port of

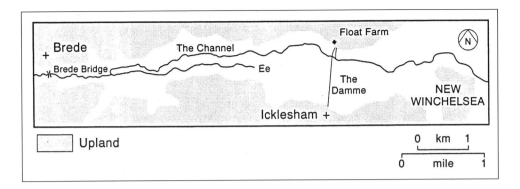

51 *Some medieval features in the Brede Level. The* Channel *was a new course dug for the river in the first half of the fifteenth century, probably in an attempt to flush silt out of the harbour to the north-east of New Winchelsea. The* Ee *was its earlier course, whose eastern end has not been traced*

New Winchelsea, which was already suffering from silting. In 1357 the king visited the port, and ordered the removal of the obstruction at *Sloughdam* (which may, or may not, have been an alternative name for the *Damme*), so that the sea should ebb and flow 'as formerly'. Later on, sometime between 1419 and 1442, a mega engineering project was undertaken further upstream. The old channel (known as the *Ee* or *Ree*, from the Old English, *ēa*, river) was abandoned, and a new channel (known simply as the *Channel*) was cut some 4.5 miles (7.5km) long, and enclosed between banks some 165 yards (150m) apart. It seems that this must have been undertaken to increase the flow of tidal water up the valley, so that the ebb could scour away the silt being deposited by the sea in Winchelsea harbour. After that time, too, it was possible for boats to navigate the river channel up as far as Brede Bridge.

There is no clear indication which side of the Isle of Oxney the Rother flowed in the early medieval period. Geological evidence suggests that it flowed round the northern side. On the other hand the county boundary, which might be expected to follow an ancient river course, runs down Wittersham Level, and documentary evidence suggests that the 'ancient' river course went that way. Be that as it may, numerous records of long-running disputes have survived to explain what happened subsequently in the Rother valleys (**52**). There, flooding occurred immediately after the disintegration of the Rye Bay barrier in the thirteenth century, and was certainly no temporary setback. It signalled an abrupt change from a period when a system of 'walls, ditches, gutters, bridges and sewers' was well-maintained to one when flooding was uncontrollable. For example, in 1290 a tenant named William Barry accused another, John Malmeyns, of refusing to repair and maintain the walls 'which he is bound to do . . . in his lands by the *sea shore* between Maytham and Newenden, whereby he and his tenants suffer *by inundation of the sea*'. In defence of John Malmeyns (who in his turn complained about the lack of action on the part of other neighbours), it should be said that he, and the others, were suddenly confronted by overwhelming difficulties. As time went on, matters only got worse. By

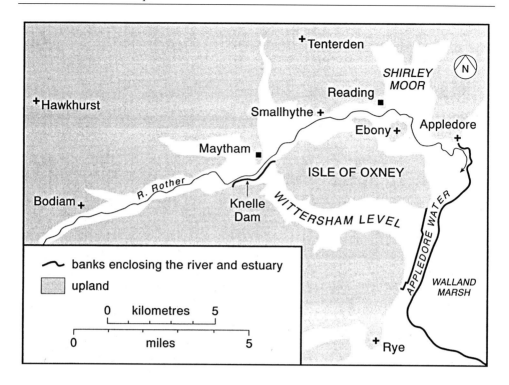

52 The course of the Rother round the north of Oxney, 1330s-1635. Soon after 1332 the Knelle Dam was built, sealing off the west end of Wittersham Level and ensuring that the river flowed round the north of the Isle of Oxney, in what became known as the Appledore Channel. The natural loops and bends of that channel would have contributed to its eventual silting up. In 1635 the Knelle Dam was intentionally breached, and the Rother allowed to flow down Wittersham Level, as it does today

1332, 650 acres (260ha) had been 'swallowed up by the sea' and more was likely to be submerged. The bridge and causeway across the levels at Newenden were threatened by the ebb and flow of the tides. For those whose memories went back that far, it must have been a depressing comparison with 50 years previously.

In the 1330s a serious attempt to improve matters was made by two local landowners, Geoffrey de Knelle (in Sussex) and Isabella Aucher of Newenden (on the Kent side). After an inquiry to discover whose interests would be damaged, permission was given for them to build a *sea wall* across the west end of Wittersham Level, on condition that the 'ancient course of the river was preserved by sufficient outlets' through it. The cost was to be borne by those who benefited from it, 'in proportion to their land holdings, their common pasture and their fisheries'. This construction, the *Knelle Dam*, was some 1.7 miles (2.7km) long and remains a very important feature of the landscape today, part of it supporting the Potman's Heath road, and part enclosing the wet level (**colour plate 21**). It is yet another surviving large-scale medieval engineering work carried out with no more sophisticated technical aids than spades and horses and carts. Its more recent history also illustrates how earlier features of marshland landscape were often adapted and later re-used for different purposes. Where possible, one generation built on the redundant works of a previous one.

However, the dam did not by any means solve all problems or satisfy all parties. It soon needed major repairs, but those who should have contributed to its upkeep failed to do so (possibly because they had not received the expected benefits), and there were accusations of collusion between the appointed inspectors and those who should have carried out the repairs. At any rate, it was reported in 1347 that 'the lands of a very great number of men' were inundated by water 'unable to find an outlet to the sea'. It therefore seems that within the short space of 15 years the main problem had changed from tidal to freshwater flooding. In the meantime, 600 acres in Wittersham Level had also been 'swallowed up' by the waters. A wall with a sluice, which may well have been Blackwall, was ordered to be built there (*see* **53**).

In 1247 those interested in navigation reacted bitterly. James de Etchingham, whose market at Salehurst near Robertsbridge depended on river transport, complained to a commission of sewers that the *Knelle Dam* was a 'great damage to the king and himself', and demanded an inquiry to see whether the dam could be removed and the flooding prevented by the ancient river walls. The Commission decided, however, that the dam was a public benefit, and furthermore it was feared that if an inquiry were set up, James would achieve his own ends by suborning the jurors.

So the *Knelle Dam* remained in place — which ensured that the Rother flowed round the north of Oxney, a course in which it stayed for 300 years. The valley was frequently flooded, but the river remained open to navigation. In the fifteenth century Smallhythe and Reading flourished as centres of shipbuilding. Henry V's warship the *Jesus* was built at Smallhythe, and Henry VII's warship the *Regent* was built at Reading and floated down to the sea past Rye as late as 1490. But, inevitably, serious silting was taking place in and adjacent to the river channel, with the result that in 1561:

> Appledore, which hath been a goodly town (is) now decayed by reason (that) the water is gone from it, and also from Reading and Smallhythe, which (used to be) always replenished with shipwrights, (where) always a great number of ships, crayers and boats were made (but) at present there cannot be made a boat of 20 tons.

The seaward end of the channel between Reading and Rye, which had formerly been 200-300ft (60-90m) wide, was reduced to only 16-24ft (5-7m) by 1562. As the channel silted up, the levels further upstream became flooded. In 1573 there was standing water at Newenden and watercourses were clogged with bull-rushes and reeds. Three thousand acres (1,200ha) upstream from Reading, known at that time as the Newenden Levels, were permanently 'drowned lands', and 2,000 acres (800ha) further downstream in Ebony, Shirley Moor and Appledore were 'summer lands', meaning that they could only be used in summer. John Stoneham's map of 1599 shows the valleys as 'Drowned Lands'.

Wittersham Level, south of the Isle of Oxney, seems to have been somewhat better off, because it was protected from freshwater floods at the west end by the *Knelle Dam* (by then also known as *Spits Wall* or *Bush Wall*), and from the sea at the east end by a wall known as the *Wittersham Sea Wall*. The Level was divided by the two causeways known as Blackwall and Kent Wall into three roughly equal parts (*see* **53**). The east end was good 'high' land which could be used all year round; the two parts to the west were lower-lying and described as 'decaying'. The Level was drained by a main sewer that flowed south to enter the tidal estuary at Scots Float.

However, around 1600 the *Knelle Dam* gave way suddenly, and it is said that two unfortunate individuals were drowned in the ensuing flood. According to a claim made in an eighteenth-century dispute, within ten days all the flood waters in the Newenden Levels had drained away into Wittersham Level. To what extent this retrospective report was exaggerated by wishful thinking we shall never know. But there is no doubt that matters improved immensely for the Newenden Levels, and they would have liked the river to continue flowing south of Oxney. Not surprisingly, the commissioners for Wittersham Level, who did not have to look far to see evidence of the troubles associated with the Rother, strenuously resisted that request. So the *Knelle Dam* was repaired and the river continued to flow round the north of Oxney.

No further steps could be taken to improve the flooding until an appropriate administrative structure had been set up. In 1609 a Commission of Sewers was issued to cover the whole river course from Bodiam, round the north of Oxney and down to a place known as *Cheriton Bars* not far north of Rye. Thus the whole river course became managed by one drainage authority, known as the Commission for the Upper Levels. An initial proposal was made to build a sluice across the river at *Thorney Wall* a mile (1.6km) downstream from Appledore, with the object of preventing the tides depositing silt further upstream and controlling the outflow of the fresh water. But that was rejected by the Lord Warden of the Cinque Ports on behalf of the mariners of Rye and Tenterden.

This was followed by a desperate, extremely expensive and, as it turned out, fruitless attempt to keep the river course open round the north of Oxney. Over £11,000 was spent, to no good effect, between 1613 and 1624. Thanks to Ambrose Cogger, an exceptionally able and methodical man who was clerk of the Upper Levels from March 1622/23, an account book has survived, giving details of income and payments, of the activities of a large workforce and the raw materials they used. The work was funded solely by the owners and tenants of land in the Upper Levels. Neither the Commissioners of Rye Harbour, who urgently needed a supply of fresh water to flush out their silted harbour, nor the tradesmen who were interested in maintaining an easy passage up the river, contributed financially. But they watched operations warily from the sidelines and complained bitterly from time to time.

The commissioners of the Upper Levels (who were the local landowners) set out in a spirit of optimism, by agreeing to levy 20 scots at a rate of 12d per acre on the deeply drowned lands (which presumably stood to benefit most) and 4d on the summer lands. Between November 1613 and September 1617 the whole length of the channel from Bodiam nearly down to Appledore was systematically dug out and widened to specified widths. The river was temporarily diverted elsewhere, and pairs of earth dams (occasionally reinforced with boards) were thrown up across the river course, so that this work could be carried out in dry conditions in one reach after another. Towpaths and their bridges were maintained in the face of very heavy construction traffic, and compensation was paid to landowners whose land was damaged. Harrows, iron rakes and an intriguing implement described as a 'porcupine' were dragged along the channel to stir up the accumulating silt. Two small indraughts (*see* glossary) were established to control the release of fresh water to flush away the silt. However, by 1621 over £6,000 had been spent in attempts to drain the valley but little, if anything, had been achieved.

The commissioners then turned their attention to two projects further downstream. First, they eventually built the freshwater sluice across the river at *Thorney Wall* that had previously been vetoed. As much material as possible was recycled. Eighty-nine tons of timber, originally parts of an indraught sluice built at Newenden, were brought down the river on lighters, to be re-built on site. It took 33 man days to load and unload it. A carpenter was paid £30, and spade work concerned with installing it cost another £80. After some debate and vacillation, no provision was made for the passage of boats, which meant that all goods passing up and down the river had to be unloaded and reloaded at the sluice: compensation was to be paid for the delay. A let-out clause was slipped in, no doubt to placate Rye: 'If the stop be hurtful to the haven of Rye or to navigation on the river, other than increasing the price of carriage, the stop shall be removed'. Whether this was ever their serious intention is very doubtful, and the sluice remained in place, eventually disintegrating around 1650.

Secondly, the commissioners decided to establish a new, vast indraught covering 200 acres (80ha) out on the Marsh between Appledore, Snargate and Fairfield. Three and a half miles (5.5km) of walls were needed: some pre-existing medieval walls were simply repaired and built higher, but other new ones had to be constructed. This was no easy task across a landscape that was deeply dissected by creeks similar to those shown on figure **5**. Creeks had to be filled in, and an access road was built. This transformation of the landscape must have been similar to that undertaken around Brookland in *c*.1200, but in this later case we have the benefit of a detailed record of the operations and expenditure. A brick sluice — a novel material — was built at the mouth of the indraught, and 7,000 bricks were brought down from Tenterden by river. In appalling conditions between spring tides and storms, two channels had to be cut across mudflats and salt marsh to the much-reduced river channel. It is doubtful how well this indraught could have operated, but anyway it had a very short life. The crunch came in the winter of 1626-7 when winds searing across the Marsh whipped up waves in the great expanse of water created by the Commissioners themselves, and broke down the walls.

This final attempt to restore the *Appledore Channel* had failed, and the Upper Levels had reached an impasse. It must have been impossible to raise any further financial support. Eventually, and with great reluctance, Wittersham Level agreed to the diversion of the Rother through their Level. Two detailed sets of arrangements were signed in 1631 and 1633. The Upper Levels agreed to undertake responsibility for all the works controlling the passage of the river through Wittersham Level which, given the problems that the river was likely to bring with it, might have seemed at the time a sure recipe for future controversy. The western two-thirds of Wittersham Level were to be used as an indraught, receiving not only the fresh water coming down the Rother but also tidal water which was admitted up an east-west channel from the *Appledore Water*. Wittersham Level simply retained rights of fishing and fowling, and taking wood and timber for their own use from that area.

The commissioners of the Upper Levels undertook to pay rent for all the land in the indraught, together with all taxes, tithes and scots. To provide a basis for this, a very detailed map of land-ownership was made, showing the exact acreage of every holding in some 1,200 acres (500ha), so that those landholders could be recompensed. In addition, agreement to the diversion had to be secured from the Lords of Romney Marsh and from the Commissioners of Walland Marsh, since the Five Waterings Sewer and the White Kemp Sewer both emptied into the tidal estuary now controlled by the Upper Levels, and might be affected by the change of river course.

By 4 May 1635 the *Knelle Dam* had been deliberately breached and the Rother was flowing down Wittersham Level. But no sooner had the diversion taken place than there was a chorus of complaints from each of the settlements further up the river, saying that navigation was 'greatly prejudiced'. The commissioners of the Upper Levels faced a very rowdy meeting in Tenterden. Thereafter there was much chopping and changing of 'pends' in the *Knelle Dam*, which controlled the level of water upstream and in the old *Appledore Channel*.

However, within ten years these new arrangements were disrupted. On Lady Day 1644 the sea once more invaded the levels, and an exceptionally high tide swept up the channels all round the Isle of Oxney. After considerable discussion, sluices were installed at Blackwall, ensuring that sea water was kept further from the Upper Levels — a move in which it is not difficult to detect self-interest on the part of landowners in the Upper Levels.

After that, and up to the 1660s, it seems that the practical drainage situation was reasonably stable and manageable. But the rents and taxes for all the drowned land in Wittersham Level had more than doubled after the 1644 sea-flood, and the Upper Levels fell seriously behind with payments. In 1664 the Wittersham Level went to the High Court to claim the £2,879 which was still unpaid. Ultimately, with the object of ending these payments, plans were made to shut the tides out of Wittersham Level entirely, leaving the area west of Blackwall as a storage area for excessive freshwater run-off (as it still is today) (*see* **53**). The Upper Levels must have felt greatly relieved: they were at last within sight of shuffling off their responsibilities in Wittersham Level, or so they must have hoped.

The contractor Richard Hudson inned land along the sides of the level, excluding the tides by earth embankments and organising the land drainage. He also shut off the former unrestricted river course down the middle of the level, and cut the brand new Craven Channel close under the Sussex hills (**53**, **54**). The efficiency of this straight canalised course, which is used by the river today, contrasted strongly with the loops and bends of the natural channel round the north of Oxney which was used before 1635.

However, after a promising beginning, hopes of a problem-free future were soon dashed by insuperable technical problems. When building the Craven Sluice, which was to let the river water out into the tidal estuary, the contractors wrote: 'at least 1,000 loads of earth (slid into the excavation), several times, one after another, and extraordinary rains, tempests and other unavoidable accidents caused great hindrances' (**colour plate 22**). A sea-flood on 5 March 1686 breached several walls and swept up into Shirley Moor. Inning of the last, central tract of the level proved very problematical and Lord Thanet a leading

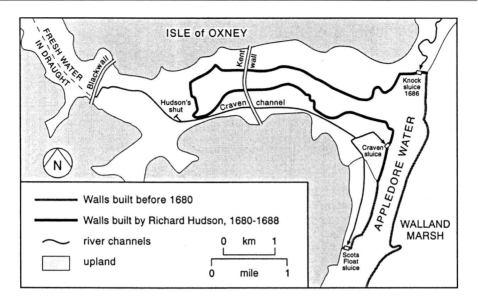

53 *Wittersham Level in 1688, after Richard Hudson's innings. He inned land along both sides of the valley, and constructed* Hudson's Shut *to divert the Rother from its previous course down the centre of the Level, and into the new* Craven Channel *which he had dug for it. Note the straightness of this channel, which would have helped the river to flow more efficiently than down the* Appledore Channel *with its curves and bends. A map of part of Hudson's innings near Craven Sluice can be seen in* **colour plate 22**

owner in Wittersham Level brought in Mark le Pla, a Huguenot immigrant living in Thorney Island in the East Anglian Fens, as an impartial consultant. He advised installing an indraught in the middle of the level, widening the Craven Channel, and using windmills which were becoming increasingly common in the Fens. However, the commissioners chose to disregard all this. Instead they employed John Nichols to build a succession of three walls across the remaining tidal area, the last of which also enclosed the upper part of the former *Appledore Water*, which is now reduced to a picturesque ditch (**55, colour plate 23**).

Within 22 years, 1,974 acres (800ha) in Wittersham Level and a further 620 acres (250ha) of the former *Appledore Water* had been reclaimed, thus greatly reducing the tidal area. Almost predictably, in 1699 the House of Commons received a petition from Rye, demanding the removal of all the new sluices and obstructions to the tides. For once, the Upper Levels and Wittersham Level were united in their opposition to this, and the petition was unsuccessful.

Otherwise no-one was satisfied. Problems became rapidly worse for all parties. Fresh water became backed up, and the Upper Levels once more became flooded, so the Craven Channel was repeatedly deepened, on the assumption that it lacked the capacity necessary to get the water away. As a result of that, its sides fell in. Worse, the peat had been reached in the deepening process, and it began to swell, break up and rise, blocking the channel. A

*54 A line of wooden posts exposed in Wittersham Level when a new pond was dug in about 1990.
Its origin is unknown, but it may be the remains of the shut (barrier) installed by Richard
Hudson some time between 1680 and 1684 to divert the Rother from its course down the centre
of the Level into the newly-dug Craven Channel. The posts survived because they were below
the water table, but were evidently damaged by the JCB digging the pond*

violent storm in December 1705 caused much damage. The sluices became clogged with
silt deposited against them by the tides when they were closed in the summer, so that they
could not be opened to allow the river water to escape in the winter. By 1730 silting had
rendered those at the head of the tidal area useless, and all the water from both the Upper
Levels and Wittersham Level had to be directed to Scots Float sluice. A double sluice was
built there, but with the outfall held up by the tides for 6 hours in every 24, that was still
not capable of getting the water away from either level. In the wet winter of 1734, a large
part of Wittersham Level was 'overflowed', and as the waters rose so did tempers. The
Upper Levels procrastinated about paying damages assessed at £426, and the bailiff of
Wittersham Level broke into the Upper Levels and seized and sold 135 of their cattle. The
matter was taken to the High Court by Wittersham Level.

To sum up, draining the river valleys was always going to be exceptionally difficult.
After the disintegration of the southern barrier in the late thirteenth century, the tides
flowed far up the valleys. But by 1500 the pendulum had swung, and the sea was in retreat.
It left behind a heightened deposit of silt, which encouraged reclamation along the sides
of the valleys — an advantage to the landowners. But it also filled channels and blocked
sluices, impeding the outflow of the rivers, and filled up the harbours. Around 1600, Rye

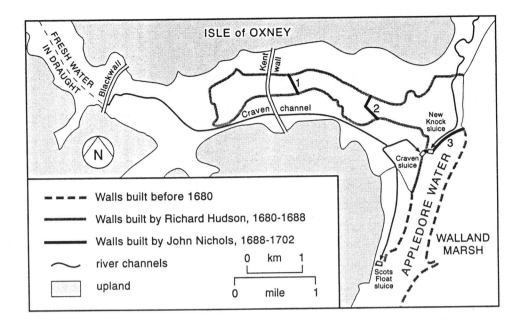

55 Wittersham Level in 1702, after John Nichols built walls 1, 2 and 3 to shut the sea out of the Level. The effect of Hudson's and Nichols' innings was to encourage silting at the head of the tidal inlet, outside the Craven and New Knock Sluices. This in turn prevented the fresh water from flowing away to the sea, and so caused flooding further up the valleys

blamed the disastrously silted condition of the harbour on the innings made in the valleys by the landowners. But in reality the reduction of tidal flow was probably almost entirely due to the natural progress of silting. Only after that had reached an advanced stage would it have been possible to inn each area of salt marsh.

This chapter highlights the fact that the needs and aims of various groups of landowners, the portsmen and those with navigational interests were so different that agreement between them was nigh on impossible. The human story lies hidden behind the administrative controversies and disputes. It is very unusual to find any information about the men who actually carried out the work, which is why the record preserved by Ambrose Cogger in the account book dealing with the fruitless attempts to keep the *Appledore Channel* open in 1613-24 is particularly valuable. It provides the names of a considerable number of the workforce, their activities and the pay they received, often for piecework. The skilled carpenters and surveyors, the experienced labourers and, on a smaller scale, the blacksmith at Sandhurst worked all year round, and sometimes all night long. Carpenters could expect up to 2s 6d a day, labourers were paid 1s 6d, and men were paid 1s a night for 'watching the dams at spring tide'. It is not hard to imagine that working conditions, always difficult, were sometimes appalling. For example, Peter Maplesden was given a sum of 5s to pay five men for working 'by night to save *Kenchill Gutt* (at Reading) from being blown up' in the winter of 1615.

Mark le Pla, probably the only observer without a personal interest in the outcome, wrote in 1689: 'I find it extremely difficult if not impossible perfectly to cure the inconveniences of the sew of these Levels . . .'. In view of what happened subsequently, how right he was. Up to the 1950s some parts of the levels were totally unproductive, and known as 'duck country'. In November 1960 the entire levels were flooded. After that, between 1966 and 1980 the banks were raised and electric pumps installed. Today, 600 acres (245ha) between the *Knelle Dam* and Blackwall are purposely set aside as a 'wet level', where excess rainwater or melted snow is stored until it can be pumped up into the river and released to the sea between high tides (**colour plate 29**). Even with that provision, on occasions such as late December 1993, on Christmas Day 1999 and again in October 2000, the whole of the Rother valley can still be flooded up to and beyond Bodiam (**colour plate 24**).

9 Rye Bay and Rye harbour

The origins of Rye Bay go back to the thirteenth century when the shingle barrier which had previously crossed from Fairlight to Dungeness broke down, allowing the tides to flow inland through a wide breach. Very rapid changes follow such a major breach, as the sea repeatedly re-orientates the beaches. Therefore all the fourteenth- and fifteenth-century beaches were lost long ago. It is likely, however, that at one time the headlands on opposite sides of the bay were as much as 3.5 miles (5.6km) apart, one lying south of Broomhill and the other south-west of Winchelsea Beach. From those positions the beaches began to grow across the inlet, advancing in a pincer movement towards Rye. At first the barriers they formed provided very extensive sheltered anchorages on which New Winchelsea and Rye flourished. But within three centuries the anchorages silted up, with disastrous results for the ports. Such is the speed of coastal change. Since the two sides of the bay developed independently, their history is described separately here. We look at the east side of the bay first, then the west side and lastly, having established a framework for them, the history of the ports.

The east side of the bay was dominated by the *westward* movement of shingle, which may seem surprising in view of the general eastward direction of longshore drift. Two local factors were responsible. First, all the time a large tidal inlet existed, the waves arriving from the south-west tended to be deflected by the movement of tidal water and so carried shingle from Broomhill westward into the inlet. Secondly, occasional winds from the east or south-east also moved shingle westwards, as they still do today. Once the shingle came to rest within the sheltered mouth of the estuary, there was no 'fetch' where the winds could create waves big enough to move it eastwards again. The quantity of shingle available was limited, and as a result of the westward movement, by about 1500 it had become so spread out that the beach had become very narrow. The sea was therefore able to roll the whole beach northward in storms. So the new barrier was migrating northward as well as moving westward.

As already described in chapter 7, the few documents available and the archaeological record of Broomhill church combine to strongly suggest that in the fourteenth and fifteenth centuries the area was protected on the south by a shingle barrier wide enough to keep the sea out. But by around 1500 that situation had changed. The sea had re-gained Broomhill, and formed a salt marsh (to set the sixteenth century in context, *see* **58**). By 1535 the tides were flowing up to the Kent Wall which was being reinforced with, among other materials, cuttings from the holly bushes growing nearby on the Dungeness shingle. The long narrow shingle barrier simply served to break some of the force of the waves offshore. Two perpetually weak points, known as the *Old Breach* and the *New Breach*, developed in the barrier and the tides flowed spasmodically in and out through them. An especially high tide would break through, helped by percolation. Longshore drift would then close up the gap. The next very high tide would break through again, and so on. The mariners of Rye had previously relied on the barrier to protect their sea-going ships anchored in the channels or drawn up in the creeks behind it, but in *c*.1570 they complained bitterly about its failure to do that. It was, they said, 'gone and worn away', and their craft were no longer safe from the 'force and rage of the sea'. They lost more in 'one foul night' than they were able 'to get up again in one whole year'. There is no doubt that the barrier was unreliable and unmanageable. At Broomhill what would be described in modern terms as a 'managed retreat' had taken place, a step backwards which might well be envied by present-day sea defence authorities. But this was probably easier to accept at that time than it would be today.

The Tudor period was, however, a time of inventiveness and adventure. Much interest was shown in 'projects' of all kinds, schemes to increase or improve agricultural land in order to produce more grain and/or meat for townspeople, and men of national standing became involved in attempts to reclaim marginal land. We have already seen that the Guldeford family carried out extensive reclamation of salt marshes in Guldeford Marsh, and their tenants crossed the *Wainway Creek* to pasture their sheep and hang up their fishing nets to dry. Owing to a disagreement about ownership they did not, however, attempt any enclosures close behind the barrier. On the other hand Armigal Wade, one of the 'projectors', did become involved. As a young man he had graduated from Oxford in 1531, and sailed off to North America taking two months to reach Cape Breton. In June 1562, by then in royal service and living in a very substantial establishment in Belsize, Hampstead, he came to Rye to muster 600 men for service at Le Havre and to collect information about likely Huguenot refugees. It must have been then that he noticed the potential, as he saw it, of the Broomhill-Camber salt marshes. Two years later, despite the unreliability of the shingle barrier, he ambitiously walled-in a vast area of 891 acres (357ha) behind it. But, and perhaps this was no surprise to the local fishermen, this innings did not last long. In October 1570 a 'great tide' overtopped the walls, washing away 150m and badly damaging another 150m of them, and breaking down and floating off a large part of the sluice. On that occasion, so we are told, 1,162 sheep were drowned. There was no attempt to re-enclose this area, possibly because Wade himself had died by then. Not until *c*.1585 was the first enduring enclosure achieved in Broomhill, this time by Customer Richard Smith of the Customs and Excise in London. He prudently took in a smaller area, some 662 acres (268ha), and set his innings back from the treacherous barrier, which may account for its success (**56, colour plate 25**). Apart from some loss along the sea front as the barrier continued to retreat, Smith's innings has survived until today, and all his walls were still standing until some were removed in the course of agricultural progress in about 1990.

The earliest accurate map of the bay, made by Philip Symondson in 1594, shows that the long but very narrow beach had then reached to within 1.3 miles (2.2km) of Rye (**57**). A composite map based on documentary evidence and knowledge of coastal processes shows the situation in the 1590s, when the whole of the Broomhill and Camber area was described picturesquely as 'a great quantity of fresh and salt marsh, stone beach and kiddle (shore-fishing) grounds' (**58**, *see* also **colour plate 25**).

56 *The view looking south-east from the site of the sluice of Richard Smith's c.1585 innings in
Broomhill, as shown on **57, 58** and **colour plate 25**. It was placed there in order that the water
from this innings should flush out the silt accumulating in the Wainway creek. A hundred years
later, when the Wainway had silted up, the flow through this sluice was reversed and the water in
the Wainway was channelled south-east, away from the camera, to reach the sea through Jury's
Gutt. The photograph also shows one of the marsh fleets, a* Phragmites *swamp which is a
welcoming haven for wildlife*

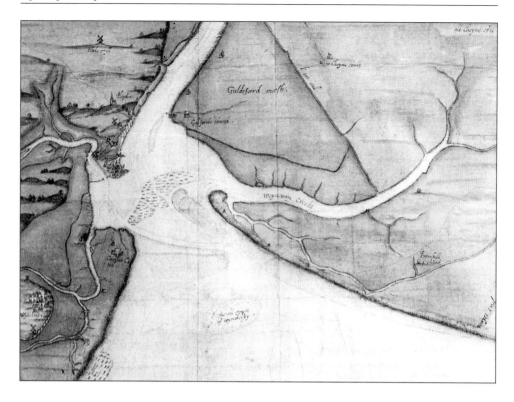

57 *Part of* The decayed harbour of Rye, *a map made by Philip Symondson in 1594, showing the two shingle headlands still 1.6 miles (2.6km) apart. The tidal* Appledore Channel *ran north, and the* Wainway Creek *ran east and then north towards Lydd. Until about 1550 the Wainway was used as a sheltered anchorage, but it was continuously reduced by silting, and in c.1570 the shingle bank which had formerly protected shipping was so low and narrow that it no longer served that purpose. Camber Castle stands isolated on the western headland, and the site of* Old Winchelsea *is marked vaguely in the middle of the bay.* ESRO ACC 6364

In 1632 the Commission of Sewers for Walland Marsh was extended to include Broomhill. This was a very important move, because it extended and defined the acreage whose tenants were contributing to the upkeep of Jury's Gutt, the outfall of the Jury's Gutt Sewer that drained the marshland west of Lydd. By around 1600 the gutt was laid through the barrier and required constant and costly maintenance. As the sea continued to roll the barrier northward, the gutt became repeatedly exposed and it had, essentially, to be an adaptable structure. It consisted of a number of wooden sections, or lengths, fitted together. Seaward sections were frequently lost in rough weather and had to be replaced by new ones on the inland side.

Then the shingle bank itself soon needed support. As the shingle continued to move away towards Rye, the beach became even thinner than before, a process no doubt accelerated by great storms in 1637, 1641 and 1648. Over time, the barrier was gradually backed up by a clay wall 'armed' with a lattice-work of faggots and timber similar to that on

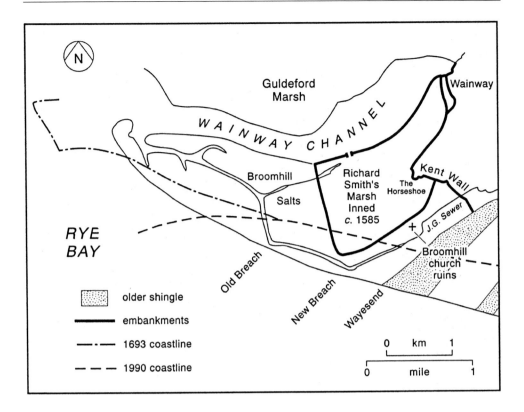

58 *In the 1590s Broomhill and Camber were described as 'a great quantity of fresh and salt marsh,*
stone beach and kiddle (shore-fishing) grounds'. The south coast was a long, narrow shingle
beach, behind which were extensive salt marshes and, north of them, the Wainway Channel.
Jury's Gutt Sewer entered the salt marshes through a sluice in the Kent Wall. From time to time
the sea broke through two breaches into that salt-marsh creek. Richard Smith's is the earliest piece
of reclaimed land to survive until today. Since then the coastline has receded northwards, and by
1693 the shingle had also extended westwards to form Northpoint Beach, now a gravel pit used
for windsurfing. Compare this with **colour plate 25**

the Dymchurch Wall. This served as an adequate protection until the 1740s. But this part of
the coast is particularly vulnerable to south-west gales, and in the winter of 1747-8 the clay
wall gave way and the sea broke in and flooded up to Scotney, more than half way to the
town of Lydd. That was an exceptionally stormy spell, and a series of great storms occurred
almost every winter until 1754, by which time the wall was in ruins. It was abandoned and
replaced in the early 1760s by a new clay wall, somewhat behind the line of the old one. That
wall, now known as the Broomhill Wall (though not the first of that name), has been
maintained for 250 years. It still consists of a clay bank, now faced with concrete. A bank of
shingle is needed in front, to ensure that the waves break some way out and to prevent the
sea from either undermining the wall or hurling shingle over the top onto the road behind.
By the mid-1950s, most of the 'natural' shingle had moved away and it had become

59 Beach-feeding in front of the Broomhill Wall in November 1983. A wide artificial bank was being built up then, but the sea was already removing some of the new shingle when it rolled down to the bottom of the slope

necessary to import more by lorry and 'feed' it to the foreshore. Now, in an average year 30,000m^3 (some 6,000 lorry-loads) are brought in from the east side of Dungeness (**59**).

The support of the Walland Marsh commission made it possible to maintain Jury's Gutt and, when the crunch came, to rebuild the sea wall in the 1760s, admittedly after considerable protests from the landowners expected to pay for it and with the help of large loans. In contrast, the coastline to the west of Richard Smith's innings (more or less the present-day sea front at Camber) did not belong in any commission because the landowners there wished to avoid paying scots. Probably as a result of that lack of official management, it had a very chequered history. First inned in 1646, it was repeatedly lost and reclaimed, and the land behind was often salted and spread with pebbles. In December 1734 a major breach occurred and rapidly widened to 275yds. This was allegedly caused by the neglect of his sea wall by the owner, Sir Charles Farnaby of Sevenoaks. Salt water flooded a large area and entered the Guldeford Sewer so that cattle refused to drink it. Other people's land was adversely affected, and patience with Farnaby ran short. Repairs to the sea wall were going to be so expensive that another managed retreat was discussed, which would have involved stepping back and using the wall on the north side of the *Wainway* as the sea wall. If that had happened, a large area of present-day sheep pasture would have been lost to the sea. Eventually, however, the wall was repaired, seemingly by the occupiers of Walland Marsh; the owners agreed to pay scots in future and

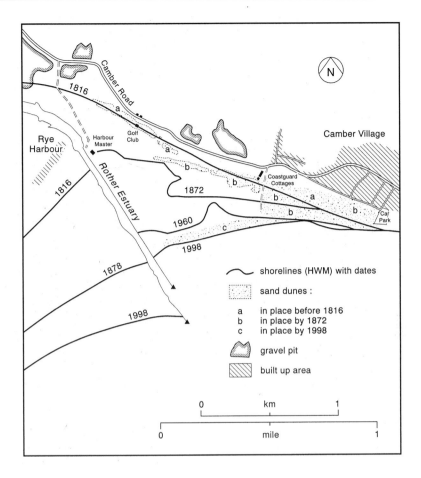

60 Land gained from the sea at Camber in the last 200 years, mainly now occupied by Rye Golf Club. There have been three main phases of dune-building

Guldeford Marsh took over the future maintenance.

The most recent additions to the east side of the bay are the Camber sand dunes, which have accumulated since about 1800 as the result of interaction between the wind and plants (**60**). Especially in winter, strong south-west winds blow onshore. When the tide is out and the wide beach dries out, the wind picks up sand grains and carries them up the beach. Anyone out there in a high wind knows how unpleasant this flying sand can be. Any low obstacle like a shingle ridge lying above the high tide mark slows the wind up, causing it to drop its load of sand and form a mini-dune. The next delivery of sand is dropped in the lee of that, building it higher. The part played by the plants is vital. Grasses with long creeping rhizomes are particularly well adapted to colonising dunes because they thrive if buried regularly by fresh supplies of sand. The primary coloniser at Camber is either sea couch grass (*Agropyron pungens*) or sand couch (*Agropyron junceiforme*). They anchor the sand and attract more. At a later stage marram grass (*Ammophila arenaria*) takes

*61 Land gained from the sea at Camber in the last 20 years. This photograph was taken looking south from the high dune south of the coastguard cottages (b on **60**). Going away on the left is the public footpath. The dune forming the horizon, which is approximately 25ft (7.5m) high and 100 yards wide at this point, has accumulated since 1979*

over. The dune grows higher, and the higher it becomes, the greater the variety of plants it supports. On the Rye Golf Club land there are three generations of dunes, for which approximate dates are given on the map. The inner one, which runs close to the road and on which the clubhouse is built, is the oldest. The one nearest the sea, which is 25ft (7.6m) high and 100m wide at the end of the path leading down from the coastguard cottages, has grown up since 1979. Thus in 20 years, the land has gained 100 yards from the sea at this point (**61**). In the public areas to the east of the golf club, less land has been gained, the lines of dunes have coalesced, and it is impossible to identify the different generations.

The shingle on the west side of Rye Bay has arrived from the south and west, the conventional direction, and it all seems to have arrived since the disintegration of the original barrier in the thirteenth century. Four distinct groups of ridges are separated by low-lying tracts of silt (**62**). The map shows that each group broadened out when it came to rest at the edge of the inlet. But so much had been lost at the south-west 'supply' end, that the ridge narrowed down to nothing and had to be replaced by a sea wall. The ridges now furthest from the sea are the earliest, the first date being provided by Camber Castle which was built near the water's edge to guard the entrance to the port (**colour plate 26**). The central tower was begun in 1512-14, and the curtain wall, bastions, and gatehouse were added between 1539 and 1543, both times when Henry VIII was on the point of war

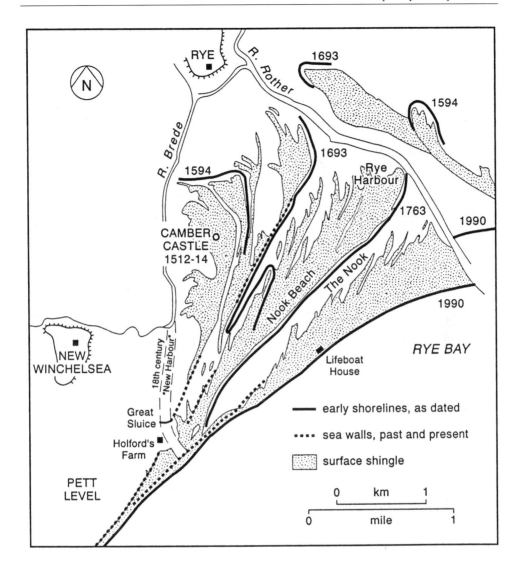

62 *On the west side of Rye Bay the coastline has been built out since 1500 by the spasmodic arrival of shingle. Very little shingle has ever crossed the current of tides flowing in and out of the Rother estuary. This map also shows the abortive eighteenth-century 'New Harbour' of Rye, and its Great Sluice*

with France. Written records show that at an earlier date, 1487, Sir Richard Guldeford had built a tower of 'stone, lime and sand . . . near the port called le Camber'. But in spite of searches by archaeologists, no trace of it has been found.

The later groups of ridges can be dated from contemporary maps, starting with Symondson's of 1594 (*see* **57**), and the last can be traced in detail on a sequence of Ordnance Survey maps. In 1873 a beach 120yds wide lay between Pett Level and the sea,

63 *The old Ship Inn, Winchelsea Beach, goes into the sea in 1931. If anyone had had a camera at* Old Winchelsea *in the thirteenth century, the scene would probably have resembled this one*

having accumulated in the lee of the Fairlight cliffs. From then onwards the sea moved that shingle progressively north-eastwards, towards the Rother, so that the bank in front of Pett Level became increasingly narrow and the remaining shingle was thrown forward onto the marshes behind. Pett Level frequently lay waterlogged in the winters. In the winter of 1931 the old Ship Inn, which had previously stood securely on the back of the shingle, was undermined and fell into the sea (**63**). Something had to be done if Pett Level was not to be perennially inundated. In the early 1930s, therefore, a pioneering method of beach-feeding was set up. A timber barrier consisting of two rows of piles 11ft (3.3m) apart boarded in along the sides was built along the front from the Lifeboat House to Cliff End (**64**). Another line of piles was sunk further out, forming a wave wall to break the force of the waves on the seaward side. The barrier was filled with shingle, a railway track was built along the top and a little petrol-driven engine pulled tipper trucks up and down the line. Using only hand shovels, the trucks were filled with shingle near the Lifeboat House, and emptied down the line wherever it was needed to replenish the barrier. This was a very expensive scheme, not least because the timber was imported from Canada. But the barrier did not last very long because the waves undermined the boarding and sucked away the shingle. It was already in a decayed state in 1940 when, because of the threat of invasion, it was deliberately breached in two places and Pett Level was flooded again, the water being contained by the bank of the Royal Military Canal in front of Winchelsea hill.

64 *Pioneering beach-feeding at Pett Level in the 1930s. This old postcard features the timber barrier of piles and boards which enclosed an artificial bank of shingle. The track of the railway which replenished the shingle runs along the top of the barrier, and the wave wall which defended the seaward side of the barrier can be seen snaking away into the distance. The cart in the picture was used to pull boats up the wooden ramp, and was nothing to do with maintenance of the barrier. Note the vertical sandstone cliffs of Cliff end in the distance*

The present Pett Wall was built of clay faced with concrete in 1947-52. More recently, it has been strengthened by additional concrete blocks at the Pett end and, in order to protect it from the force of the waves and prevent the sea throwing shingle over the road, every year an average of 30,000m³ per year of shingle is 'fed' by lorry to the front of it.

Some ten years after that wall was built, cuttings in the surface of the offshore peat were noticed (**colour plate 5**). At that time there was even a pyramid of peat stacked up, ready to be carted away. Evidently the peat-cutters never returned to collect it. Possibly they had, for some unknown reason, to leave the area in a hurry. The cuttings extend for at least 2 miles (3km) along the foreshore, showing that peat-winning was a major local industry. Its date is not known, but is likely to have been medieval, when it may have been supplying fuel for salt-working.

The two evolving headlands provided essential shelter for the harbours of New Winchelsea and Rye. Basically fishing ports, they had the immense economic advantage of commanding the shortest Channel crossing to Normandy, and on to Paris. And they had, for a time at least, a capacious haven. Fishing and maritime trade, both across the Channel and along it, were therefore their life-blood. In addition, during the Hundred Years War, especially in the early decades of the fifteenth century their harbour known as the Camber or *La Chambre* was used as an assembly point for large numbers of men and quantities of supplies to be taken across the Channel.

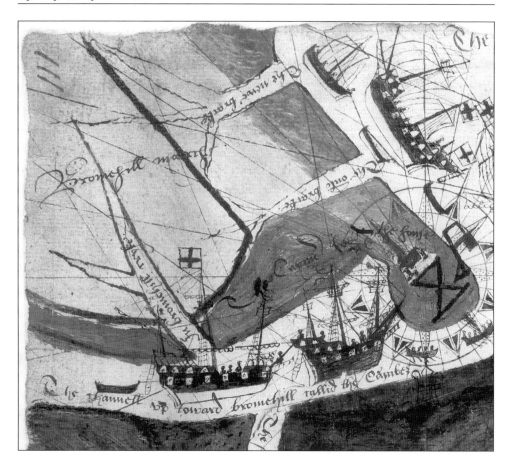

65 Big ships and little men. Since the fourteenth century shipping had been anchoring in the Camber, but by the time this pictorial map was made by John Prowez in c.1572 that had just about come to an end. However, his picture of ships anchored stem to stern and reached by ladders from small rowing boats also gives us an insight into how shipping may have lain in earlier centuries in the tidal inlet at Romney. This map was drawn with north at the bottom, and this extract shows the Camber shore (with the two breaches) slanting from the centre top toward the bottom right; the 'Channel up toward Broomhill called the Camber', and Broomhill Marsh in between them. PRO MPF 212

In the second quarter of the sixteenth century, New Winchelsea ceased to function as a port of any significance (*see* page 98) and Rye, which was already a substantial port, prospered at her expense (**65**). Rye's population reached a peak of around 5,000 in the 1550s and '60s, but then it too declined. From 1580 onwards that decline was very rapid, and a population of 4,000 in 1580 was reduced to 2,000 by 1600. The causes of this spectacular downturn were complex. The maritime trade depended to a large extent on providing vast quantities of firewood and other provisions, mainly foodstuffs, to Boulogne and Calais, remaining English outposts on the French coast. In some years up to 300 ships left the port in that direction. But Boulogne was lost in 1550 and Calais in 1558. Almost overnight, Rye lost three-quarters of its trade, and all supporting industries suffered a knock-on effect. For a different reason the fishing industry also suffered badly. It had formerly depended mainly on the London market because, perhaps surprisingly, fish caught at Rye in the morning could be carried by road and sold in the capital later the same day. But the London market failed and so fishing went into steep decline from 1580 onwards. Numerous people left the town in search of an alternative livelihood.

The primary reasons for Rye's decline were thus political and economic, but the inevitable problem of silting followed not far behind. Pulling together the strands of what has been said already elsewhere, the *Appledore Water* up to Reading was a fraction of its former width, a large area of Guldeford Marsh had been reclaimed, and the *Wainway* was much reduced. In addition, parts of the Tillingham valley, upstream from the Strand, were walled in. This large reduction of the area covered by the tides meant that there was much less to carry away the silt on the ebb. Credit must go to Armigal Wade for anticipating the adverse effect of silting somewhat earlier than most other people, and attempting a scheme to 'amend the Camber'. In *c*.1564 he tried to harness the tidal water entering through one of the breaches in the Broomhill-Camber barrier and divert it round through the *Wainway* to scour away the silt accumulating there. Unfortunately the experiment was a total failure, as the sea simply came in at one breach and flowed out at the other (another example of how the barrier was unmanageable). So silting continued unabated, and its effects on shipping are well illustrated by replies to an inquisition taken in 1619. It was said that 50 years previously, flat-bottomed boats of 5 or 6 tons had gone up the *Wainway* to unload goods destined for Lydd at the place called *Wainway* (*see* **58**); that up to 60 ships of 80-100 tons could anchor between Camber Point and Guldeford at the mouth of the *Wainway*; and that 20 ships 'of good burden' could be anchored near Camber Castle. But by 1619 none lay in any of these places.

Rye's reaction, at a time when its funds were already very scarce, was to spend vast sums on schemes to improve its harbour. In the 1590s channels were restricted, a Great Sluice was built across the Tillingham, and diversion of the Rother round the north of the town and into the Tillingham was discussed. All these aimed to intensify the effect of the ebb tide, and all failed. Considerable sums were also paid to Frederico Genebelli, an Italian, for drawing up a scheme quite beyond the town's means. That was dropped immediately it became clear that he proposed to cut a new channel to the sea at Winchelsea Beach, because that would have benefited Winchelsea rather than Rye (*see* **57**). These projects effectively bankrupted the town.

Throughout the seventeenth century Rye continued to protest vigorously about the possible ill-effects of reclamations and alterations in management of the Rother upstream, though with little or no power to do anything about them. It did not, however, concern itself with final stages of reclamation of the *Wainway* channel, presumably because there was no longer any hope of boats anchoring there. On the other hand the *Wainway* is of very great interest to archaeologists and landscape historians. Between 1600 and 1700 a succession of six walls were built across this narrow tidal inlet, progressively reclaiming a total of 1,300 acres (420ha). Eventually the Wainway Sewer silted up beyond recall, and alternative arrangements had to be made for its drainage (*see* **56**). Because this area was reclaimed so recently an exceptionally full documentary record of those activities survives, and because a large part of the area has never been ploughed the walls and some sites of sluices, together with numerous fossil watercourses, remain in the landscape. Here, then, is an area that offers a very unusual opportunity to explain, and date, a landscape of reclamation using contemporary documents, and to work out how the reclamation was actually carried out. This should provide important clues as to how other extensive areas of Walland Marsh were reclaimed in earlier centuries, for which no such combination of landscape and documents survives. A study which involves recording this landscape in great detail and searching through numerous seventeenth-century documents is under way.

The town of Rye did not easily forget its former prosperity, and one last attempt was made to restore its fortunes, by building a completely new harbour. In 1724 the commissioners of Rye Harbour obtained an Act of Parliament 'for restoring the harbour of Rye to its ancient goodness'. The remarkable thing is that the plan seems very similar to that of Genebelli, which Rye had rejected out of hand 125 years previously. It involved cutting a gently-curving channel leading in from the sea at Winchelsea Beach up to, but not connecting with, the elbow of the river Brede below Winchelsea hill (*see* **62**). Detailed infrastructure was put in place; staff were appointed, a bank loan accepted, and land was purchased. Expensive materials were bought, down to 30 wheelbarrows for removing the shingle. Since the site was still very remote, a new road had to be built from Rye and a carpenter employed to build a bridge over the Brede and Tillingham channels. By 1734 two elegant pier heads and a Great Sluice had been built of Portland Stone, and the channel was partially lined on both sides with timber piles, planking and staging. But by then there were already structural and financial problems. In 1748 the project came to a standstill, £11,000 in debt. In 1762 the sea was let in and the channel immediately filled with silt. John Smeaton, famous for building harbour installations and bridges, was consulted. He made detailed suggestions for diverting all three rivers so that they reached the sea through the new channel, in order to remove the deep deposit of silt. Some of the necessary engineering work was put in place but this, of course, upset established and already difficult drainage arrangements in the marshes. Problems got worse. Silt filled the channel, shingle moved across the mouth, and the Great Sluice was ruinous. In spite of growing threats of public disorder, the harbour was eventually opened in June 1787 'with lights by night and flags by day'. At a meeting in the Court Hall in Rye on 6 November it was declared that every possible experiment had been tried, the new harbour was 'totally inadequate' for navigation, it upset the drainage of most of Walland Marsh, and it was concluded that the 'ancient harbour is more safe and commodious for shipping'. So, after 63 years, the 'New Harbour' was abandoned. But it has left its imprint on the landscape. The two banks support lines of houses, Willow Lane crosses the harbour at the site of the Great Sluice, the impressive Portland Stone structure of the east pier can sometimes be seen on the beach after a storm has removed some of the beach, and the wooden extensions of both piers jut out into the sea (**66**).

To sum up, since the breakdown of the original barrier across the bay in the thirteenth century, shingle has always been in short supply. Two new barriers grew out from opposite sides, but as that shingle moved in towards the centre of the bay, so the 'feeder' ends of

66 *The pier heads of the eighteenth-century abortive 'New Harbour' of Rye, at Winchelsea Beach.
In the foreground is the elaborate Portland Stone work of the East Pier Head with, behind part
of the 1930s wave wall, its wooden extension jutting out to sea. The stonework of the West Pier
Head is missing, its wooden extension can just be seen behind a groyne on the right of the picture.
Although this is known locally as 'Smeaton's Harbour', in fact John Smeaton was only consulted
once, and that was only after the project had already been going for 40 years*

those beaches became seriously depleted. By *c.*1500 the barrier on the east side of the bay,
derived from shingle which stayed behind and did not go off to build up Dungeness, was
so narrow that it was being rolled inland, and a slice of land possibly a mile (1.6km) wide
was lost along that front before it was stabilised around 1750. Deposits on the west side of
the bay are both shallow and discontinuous, showing that the quantity which has entered
the area from the direction of Fairlight since the thirteenth century has been very limited.

In the last 750 years far greater changes have taken place in Rye Bay than on any other
part of the Romney Marsh coastline, to which the inhabitants have been forced to adapt
very frequently. Considering that Rye is now 2.5 miles (4km) by river from the open sea,
and New Winchelsea an additional 1.5 miles (2.5km), it is clear that in the long term the
inhabitants have been more successful in building sea walls than they were in preventing
silting of their ports.

10 Continuing change

This chapter brings the story up to date, first inland and then on the coast. Land drainage is one of the two keys to the continuing occupation and use of the Marsh. Before 1800, all the water in the channels on the Marsh either reached the sea through sluices set in the sea walls or, in the case of the Five Waterings Sewer and the White Kemp Sewer, emptied into the Rother estuary. Then, Napoleon's threatened invasion provided the area with a very valuable additional waterway — the Royal Military Canal — and some of the water could be directed backwards, as it were, into the canal (**67**).

The problems of draining the marshland are, as they always have been, rooted in the fact that most high tides rise to levels significantly above those of the marsh, so that the fresh water can only flow out to sea when the tide is low. The Appledore Dowels, the Cheyne and Fairfield are exceptionally low-lying areas which have always been particularly difficult to drain. In historic time the Dowels often lay under water, useless. In *c*.1620, for example, no scots were paid on them and they were simply described as 'certain wet lands, containing by estimation 4 or 500 acres . . . which always winter and summer lie drowned . . .'. The reasons for the flooding were that the marshland between the Dowels and the Five Waterings Sewer was higher than those 500 acres (200ha), and that several streams continually brought water down from the adjacent hills. Now their water is pumped into the canal and they can be used year round as sheep pasture.

It is worth considering, in the light of past history, *why* these particular areas are so low-lying. In each of them the peat is very near the surface and only covered by a relatively thin layer of sediment. In other words, the tides can only have flowed over them for a short period of time since the peat was formed. How did that come about? In *c*.AD200, when the sea flowed in over most of the peat platform, all these areas were a long distance from the open sea and so were overflowed less frequently than other places. Later, when the sea advanced from the south in the thirteenth century, these areas were again out of reach, this time because they were protected by the *Great Wall*. Thus, thanks to successful medieval sea defence, the peat remained near the surface and later on this was the cause of very considerable difficulties. It will be remembered that the peat has only been preserved because it has remained *below* the water table. Therefore, attempts to drain these areas, both in the past and at present, have encountered problems. The peat is like a sponge with a high water content. Land drainage, designed to lower the water table, removes that water, with the result that the peat shrinks. More importantly, when it is exposed to the air, chemical and biological decay set in. It is quickly oxidised, and then attacked by bacteria, fungi and animal organisms, and literally disappears into thin air. This loss of substance, known as peat wastage, lowers the land-surface still further, and increases the drainage problems. 'Successful' drainage of land where peat is near the surface thus begins

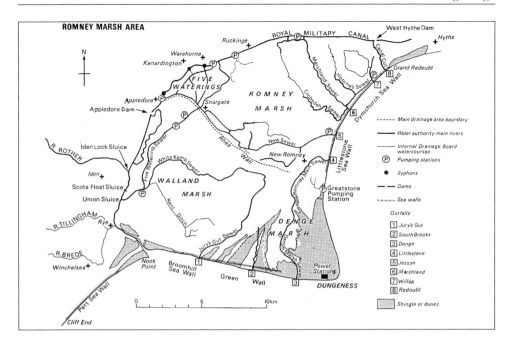

67 *Map of present-day drainage of the Marsh. This shows the ancient sewers leading to outfalls placed in the sea walls or, in the case of the Five Waterings Sewer and the White Kemp Sewer, into the lower reaches of the Rother, as well as the much more recent pumps taking the water up into the Royal Military Canal. The Appledore Dowels are in the area marked 'Five Waterings'*

a vicious cycle. Further drainage causes further wastage, and so on. Not only that, but wastage also involves loss of the upper layers of the peat, which implies irretrievable loss of part of the environmental record. The logs and tree trunks, known generally inaccurately as 'bog oaks', do not waste away, and so stay on top of the remaining peat. Occasionally they block the sewers and ditches and have to be removed (**68**, see also **20**).

The difficulties of draining and the implicit threat of flooding of such land mean that houses were very seldom built there — note the blank spaces on the maps of the Dowels and the Cheyne, which are devoid of human habitation and roads. Fairfield church, perched on the more solid foundation of the silts of an early creek, occasionally becomes an island surrounded by flooded 'peat land' (**colour plate 27**). The hazard of building in such a situation is illustrated by Hazelden House, not far from the Woolpack Inn, south of Brookland. That house was built on the side of an unnamed wall, a secondary rampart some 600yds behind the *Great Wall*. The adjacent field has evidently subsided, tilting the older part of the house away from the wall. A later addition (between the two chimneys) appears to be propping up the older part of the building (**colour plate 28**).

The river valleys are similar low-lying land, liable to flooding and almost without human habitation. There the underlying peat has caused, and is still causing, yet another problem. The Rother Area Drainage Improvement Scheme carried out between 1966 and 1980 included raising the banks of the Rother and its major tributaries, as well as installing

68 A 3,000 year-old 'bog oak' being pulled out of a drainage channel in the Appledore Dowels by tractor. Land drainage has caused wastage of the upper layers of the peat, so that the logs become concentrated at the surface and, as the level of the land is also lowered, they tend to block the passage of water. Although traditionally described as bog oaks, analysis of pollen from the surrounding peat has shown that these trees were probably alders

pumping stations (**colour plate 29**). The object was to ensure that the river water would stay within the banks, and not over-top them except in the 'wet level'. However, the weight of the banks themselves compacts and depresses the peat. The result is that they subside and need constant maintenance and topping up if they are to contain the river when in flood. Similarly, the pumping stations also 'sank' into the peat. Thus, all the areas where the peat is near the surface can only be satisfactorily drained if their water is pumped into channels at a higher level, and even with that provision, there are ongoing problems.

Although Napoleon never landed, he certainly left his mark on the Marsh. Every visitor coming to the Marsh by land has to cross the Royal Military Canal or one of the connecting rivers, and very few can fail to notice them (**69**). Mostly completed between Seabrook and Iden between December 1804 and July 1806, the structure consisted of a 60ft (18.3m) wide trench, with the spoil piled up into a defensive rampart on the landward side. Behind that was a military road and, at the very back, a wide ditch which collects the water from the upland streams interrupted by the canal. The system was completed by a towpath on the marsh side (**70**). The structure can best be seen between Warehorne and Iden, although south of the Appledore Dam a bank has been added on the Marsh side to

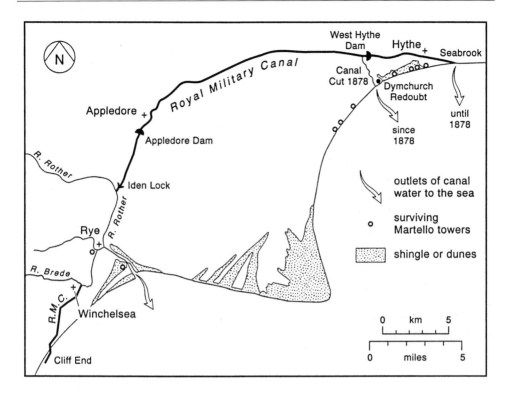

69 A map of the Royal Military Canal, showing its outfalls before and after 1878

increase its capacity as a reservoir. Elsewhere, although the waterway still exists, the parapet, military road and towpath have been largely destroyed by ploughing.

As a reservoir, the canal serves two highly important functions. It is an integral part of the drainage system, and it provides water for agriculture, which was exactly what William Pitt, the Prime Minister, suggested with remarkable prescience when trying to placate the farmers whose fields and farms were cut in two in 1804. Since Pitt's time, the system has been somewhat modified. The Canal Cut was dug in 1878 to bring the canal water to the sea through the Dymchurch Wall south of the Grand Redoubt, a shorter route than via the sluice at Seabrook (*see* **colour plate 8**). In 1883 the West Hythe Dam was built below the Roman fort at Stutfall, effectively blocking off the east end of the canal, which Hythe then purchased. A dam has also been added south of Appledore.

Each of the three rivers has a tidal sluice designed to prevent the salt water flowing upstream and to allow the fresh water to flow out to sea when required. Those on the Brede and Tillingham are just above the Strand Quay at Rye, and the Scots Float Sluice on the Rother is 1.6 miles (2.5km) upstream from its confluence with the other two rivers at Rye. In summer the sluices on the rivers and the coast are mostly kept closed, and very little water is released to the sea. Almost all the rain and river water is retained for the 'wet fences', the name given to the watercourses which serve to separate the stock in adjacent fields, and for the benefit of the crops now grown on the Marsh, not least the thirsty

70 The Royal Military Canal at Appledore, looking south. On the right is the rampart built with the spoil dug out of the canal, on which a WWII blockhouse is perched. The photograph was taken from the road to Fairfield, which follows the original tow path for some 250 yards

potatoes. The main source of water for the canal reservoir is the Rother system. In summer it is taken in from the river at Iden Lock and also from the Reading Sewer just south of the Appledore Dam, and can then be passed through that dam and gravity-fed into the Marsh channels. The water which comes down into the canal from the hills behind Hythe is also a potential resource for Marsh agriculture, and arrangements have been made to transfer it westward past the West Hythe Dam in summer. Other streams from the surrounding upland are either diverted into the canal or siphoned under it and out onto the Marsh.

In winter surplus rainwater is pumped from the marsh channels into the canal, and reaches the sea by way of the Canal Cut. Initially the necessary power for draining the Dowels was provided by windmills. In 1852 the first steam pump was installed, and in 1949 steam was replaced by diesel-powered pumps. After a spell of wet weather the water can be seen gushing forth into the canal at the Appledore Pumping Station, where the B2080 turns east away from the canal. Therefore, perhaps unexpectedly, the canal is likely to be full in summer (the dry season) and less full in the winter, except after very heavy rain.

In the past 60 years or so the economy, and hence the landscape, of the Marsh has undergone a great transformation. In 1939 nine-tenths of the whole area was permanent pasture, grazed by some 200,000 sheep, and apart from the addition of later innings, the landscape can have been little different from that of the fifteenth century when it became pasture. There, sealed in by the grass, was a historic record going back certainly to medieval and possibly, in parts, to Saxon times. Then the scene began to change. During the war the Marsh farmers were directed to plough up one-third of their land. At first progress was slow, not least because they did not have the appropriate machinery, but by 1945 over 12,400 acres (5,000ha), or 35%, had been ploughed, and that demonstrated the potential success of local arable farming. From 1950 increasing areas were ploughed, and after 1975 the rate of ploughing speeded up. Now less than 10% of the whole area consists of permanent pasture. This had a knock-on effect on where people lived. As recently as 1970 scattered farmhouses were still occupied, well away from the roads; now most of them have been abandoned. And in the course of this agricultural revolution, a great deal of the historic landscape, an important resource for historians, has been lost (**71**).

On the coastline, which is the other key to the survival of the Marsh, two areas have recently been gaining ground from the sea. As already described, part of the Camber dunes has advanced some 750yds in 200 years, and is continuing to do so. Extensive gains have also been made to the east of New Romney, though since that area is sheltered from the prevailing winds and waves by Dungeness, the changes have been relatively slow and quiet. To recap, nearly a thousand years ago Romney became, for perhaps only a couple of centuries, a very important port based on an extensive sheltered inlet. That inlet silted up,

71 Sandyland, Broomhill, in an abandoned state in 1980. It has now gone altogether, typical evidence of the rural depopulation which has occurred on the Marsh since about 1970. An old sea bank this side of the house was demolished in about 1990 and an adjacent field was converted from sheep pasture to crops

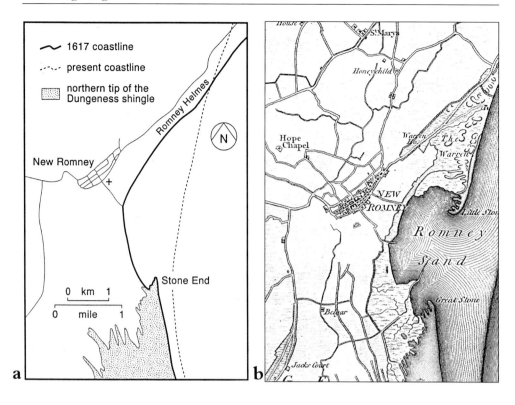

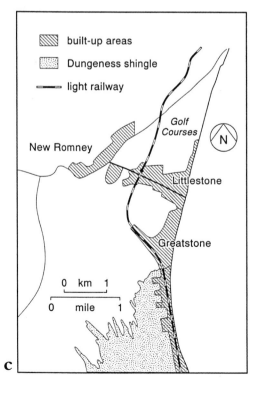

72 The progressive retreat of the sea from New Romney, 1617 – 1999

a) 1617 coastline, as shown Matthew Poker's map.

b) 1816 coastline on the first edition of the one-inch Ordnance Survey.

c) New Romney, Littlestone and Greatstone in 1999.

Considering the high density of housing in Littlestone, it may be difficult to believe that much of that area was washed over by the tides less than 200 years ago and ever since the thirteenth century the sea has been slowly retreating. Now the town is over a mile (2km) from the sea, no waterway passes it, and no landscape evidence points to where the harbour may have been. The early maps are no help in providing detail on Romney, because by *c.*1600 it was a shrunken town, and was not a focus of interest. Poker's map of 1617 simply illustrates a slight bay between a shingle headland on the south known as *Stone End*, which was the northern extremity of the Dungeness shingle, and low sand hills known as the *Romney Helmes* to the north-east (**72a**). Around 1800 a small quantity of shingle moved south from the Dymchurch Wall and formed an outer barrier called *Little Stone* (**72b**). This small but important barrier created a sheltered area behind it where silting took place, following the pattern of evolution which had occurred elsewhere, on a much larger scale, earlier in the history of Romney Marsh. Without the *Little Stone* spit, the Romney coastline would in all probability have remained a shallow, sandy embayment until today. As it was, in 1839 a wall was built to exclude the sea from what is now the northern half of Littlestone golf course. Fishermen drove their carts along a causeway, a 'wagon road', which led across the sands from the north end of New Romney to the tip of *Little Stone* but became submerged at high tide. The gap between the tips of Littlestone and Greatstone was never naturally closed. Around 1900 a sea wall was built along that front, and amid much modern development the wagon road of 1839 has become the main road from New Romney to the sea front (**72c**). The Littlestone Wall was built in the 1970s, and protected by a bank of imported shingle, which is now topped up from lorries when necessary.

Further north, the Dymchurch Wall continued to be maintained, year in, year out, and survived various crises, notably in the 1620s, 1705, 1803 and 1890. In the 1820s the clay and woodwork structure was reinforced for the first time by rocks, and although the clay core is now faced with various combinations of rock and concrete, it still needs constant maintenance (**73**). Most recently, 1.6 miles (2.4km) at the north end of the wall was raised by about 1ft (0.3m) in the 1970s, and the 1.3 miles (2km) south of Dymchurch was rebuilt in the late 1990s.

The Dungeness mass is by far the largest remaining fragment of the original shingle barrier, and the southern shore, between Broomhill and Dungeness, takes the full force of south-west gales. The shingle there is moved in two directions. First, the waves carry large quantities along the coast to Dungeness by the process of longshore drift, and deposit it on the east coast. As a result, the south coast of Dungeness is losing ground, and the east coast is being built outwards by the addition of new shingle ridges. At the same time, the southern shore is also being 'rolled' inland, especially in the great storms. Whenever an onshore gale coincides with a high spring tide, water percolates through the sea bank, carrying pebbles with it. The water usually seeps back into the sea when the tide goes out. But in the great storms so much water comes in that unless attempts are made to prevent it doing so it would flow up to the town of Lydd. So perhaps it is not surprising that historical records show that from a very early date clay banks were built in attempts to keep the floodwater down near the sea. The present defence is the Green Wall, which was built in two stages, being started in the west in the 1880s, and extended eastwards during the First World War (*see* **67**). To a considerable extent it restricts potential flooding, but it cannot be effective under all conditions. In great storms a very large volume of water

73 One of the older parts of the Dymchurch Wall, north of Dymchurch, where it is faced with a mixture of stone and concrete. The sea targets all the weaknesses, so this structure is in constant need of patching

builds up, exerting great pressure on the wall and percolating through the shingle beneath it. Equally, it may break through the wall at any weak point. With the current emphasis on 'environmental' interests, badgers are protected, and rabbits are rife. Both species live in the Green Wall, with the result that there are plenty of weak points in it. It was breached in March 1990, and again in October 1999, starting on both occasions at animal burrows (**colour plate 30**). This spasmodic flooding of the MoD ranges between Lydd and the coast, and of Denge Marsh, can be expected to continue (**74**).

Dungeness has many attractions. It is the first landfall for large numbers of migratory birds; it supports an exceptional flora and fauna, in recognition of which it was designated a National Nature Reserve in 1998; and it is relatively remote. For that last reason it was chosen in the late 1950s as the site for one of the new generation of Magnox nuclear power stations. At the public enquiry that preceded it, an academic geographer gave evidence that the south coast was migrating northwards. Nevertheless, power stations need to be built in close proximity to a copious supply of cooling water, and the sea is deep to the south of the point and shallow on the east side of it. For that reason, and on account of the number of bungalows on the east side, the Dungeness A power station was sited near the south coast. In a short space of time the erosive powers of the sea became apparent and beach-feeding started at the front of the Power Station in 1966. By 1979, 26,700m³ of shingle was being brought back annually from the east side of the point and tipped on the seaward site of the power station. In the mean time a second power station, Dungeness B, was built to

74 *Paddling Pylons. Two sets of transmission lines lead away from the Dungeness power stations, across Denge Marsh. The shingle bank defending the south side of Denge Marsh is weak, so that this area is particularly liable to flooding*

the west of Dungeness A (**colour plate 31**). In the great storms of 1990 the sea lapped at the gates of the compound of Dungeness A, and flooded into that of the switching station to the west of Dungeness B. In order to try and prevent the sea advancing further, a huge bank of shingle has now been built up in front of the stations. This will have to be replenished and the recycling operation will have to be continued until both stations can finally be safely disposed of, which will probably be in over 100 years time. In the mean time, as the rest of the coastline to the west of the power stations retreats northwards, the power stations will become increasingly vulnerable, projecting out into sea.

For several thousand years Romney Marsh developed behind a vast, stable barrier, which received enough natural replenishment from the south-west to maintain that stability (*see* **14**). Then the supply of shingle diminished and the barrier began to break down. That legacy of the Ice Age was running out, and the beaches were running short of shingle. Now four sea walls link the remaining blocks of shingle in a defensive cordon, without which the sea would flow in over the Marsh. The maintenance of most of the walls themselves depends on artificial replenishment of shingle by beach-feeding. Thus, with the exception of the Camber sand dunes and the Dymchurch Wall, the whole of the Romney Marsh coastline is dominated by movement of shingle. Beach-feeding, bringing the shingle back from wherever the sea deposits it, is an essential local industry which will have to be continued as long as the Marsh is occupied.

The Marsh has long been reclaimed and defended against the sea, expertly, painstakingly and expensively. Its survival depends on constant and continuing maintenance of both the land drainage system and the sea defences. Advances in technology have to some extent changed the means by which this is achieved. For instance, maintenance of clay walls covered with a lattice-work of timber products has been replaced by seasonal recycling of shingle by lorries. Also, over the last 20 years the perceived importance of 'environmental' concerns has increased considerably, though in some ways sea defence and environmental interests do not coincide. No engineer needs badgers tunnelling into the clay sea walls for which he is responsible!

The paradox, noted several times already, is that the more successful the sea defences, the more difficult it is to drain the land protected by them. The Marsh is, in Camden's frequently-quoted phrase, 'the gift of the sea' — it was built up by the tides bringing in sediments. But for centuries past the inhabitants have done their best to exclude the tides, and in doing so they also excluded the gift of sediment. As medieval men kept out the waters, so we are doing today. Now, with some 30,000 permanent residents living along the coastal fringe, swollen to 50,000 in the summer season, the combination of sea defence and land drainage will have to be maintained, but the process will become increasingly difficult and expensive.

11 Conclusion

As recently as the late 1970s very little was known about either the geological evolution or the human history of Romney Marsh. The radical and sometimes very rapid changes that had taken place in both the coastal and inland environments in historic and prehistoric time were not appreciated. Therefore the close interplay between those and human occupation and activities had not been questioned. At that time it was clear to a few geologists, and probably to them alone, that the Marsh had been built up, one layer of sediment upon another, over several thousand years, but in spite of that the exciting possibility of buried archaeological horizons was not yet recognised. The historical significance of the wealth of landscape features had hardly been considered. Local historical interest centred on the ports. Four of these, described so brilliantly by Kipling as 'ports of stranded pride', had obviously silted up centuries ago. Another, *Old Winchelsea*, had been lost to the sea. But it was scarcely known when, and certainly not how or why this happened.

Twenty years ago, stimulated by scientific and public interest in changing sea level coupled with an increasing awareness of the excitement of the local history, the spotlight began to focus on the Marsh. Since then detailed and wide-ranging studies have been conducted by scientists, archaeologists and historians. This work has been promoted and supported by the Romney Marsh Research Trust, which has also provided an essential forum for coordination between the very different fields of expertise. As a result, Romney Marsh is now one of the best understood of all the English marshlands. A huge amount of information has been collected and analysed, using scientific techniques never previously used on the Marsh. The underlying sediments have been intensively studied through the microfauna they contain, the grain sizes of the different layers, and especially by analysing the record of the pollen preserved in the peat. As a result of this, a picture has been built up of the various sedimentary sequences in different parts of the Marsh, and the environments under which those sediments were deposited during the last 6,000 years. This is now backed up by an extensive database of radiocarbon dates, which provides a chronology of those evolving environments wherever datable, organic material is present.

Seismic technology has been used to throw light on evidence which lurks unseen. Offshore, a high-resolution geophysical survey, able to penetrate the sea bed to a depth of between 65-100ft (20-30m), was undertaken to look for signs of the barrier which once crossed Rye Bay. That was not found, but the early relationship between the coast and the English Channel was examined. At Broomhill a resistivity survey was used in 1985 to locate the outline of the walls of the medieval church buried some 2ft (60cm) underground. This was the first buried feature to be explored. With a succession of sedimentary layers lying one upon another, it became clear that more archaeological evidence was likely to be buried. The problem was, and still is, finding it. More recently, however, archaeological surveillance in advance of gravel extraction in Lydd Quarry has led to the discovery of buried land-surfaces of four very different periods — Early Bronze Age, Late Iron Age, Roman and Medieval. The discovery there of a buried medieval landscape, complete with artefacts by which to date it, is exceptional even by national standards. On Romney Marsh proper an occupied Roman land-surface is buried about 3ft (1m) below the surface.

Romney Marsh has a remarkable legacy of medieval earthworks including ditches that form the boundaries of numerous small fields and tracks, sites of moated houses and mill-banks. This rich and unusual inheritance exists because, following intensive farming in the twelfth to fourteenth centuries, the area was depopulated, and when it became permanent pasture in the fifteenth century, all the earlier features were grassed over. They remained under that carpet of grass until extensive ploughing began some 40 years ago. A selection of those which had survived the onward march of the plough until the 1990s have been surveyed and recorded in detail. On some of the fields which have been ploughed, field walking has been carried out — a much cheaper exercise than excavation, and one which can cover a much wider area. Recent re-excavation and assessment of all possible detail on the site at *Sandtun*, West Hythe has shown that it is the first Middle Saxon settlement to be identified on the south or east coast of England which was trading with the Continent but was not a permanently settled town.

Gordon Ward's initiative in relating historic documents to the landscape has been followed, 50-60 years later, by the unravelling of the medieval reclamation history of Misleham, on Walland Marsh. At present, similar but even more detailed work is being undertaken in the *Wainway*, relating a very full documentary record to the landscape, also almost intact, in an area progressively gained from the sea in the seventeenth century. Similar research has been carried out in the Rother valleys, dealing with the critical seventeenth-century period when the river was diverted from north to south of the Isle of Oxney. Through that a partial understanding of historic river-management has been built up, though much more still needs to be explained.

On the basis of what has been achieved in the last 20 years it is possible to sum up the Romney Marsh story as it is understood at present. Human occupation and activities were dominated by a constantly changing environment. Around 6,000 years ago shingle began to enter this area from the south-west, and in a short space of time built out a massive barrier from Fairlight across a sandy bay as far as the later position of Dymchurch. This was the youthful, enthusiastic phase in the life of the barrier, when changes probably took place very rapidly. From then onwards the barrier was fundamental to the history of the Marsh, dominating both physical evolution and human occupation. By the second millennium BC, Early Bronze Age men were on the barrier, apparently using it as a stopping-off point on a trade route across the Channel to the Continent. They also used the flint shingle to make weapons for hunting. In the meantime, the rise in sea level had caused a back-up of river water in the valleys, with the result that freshwater fen developed and continued there for several thousand years. Simultaneously, the tides continued to flow round the north end of the barrier into the lagoon, depositing sediments there faster than sea level rose. As the lagoon became shallower, salt marsh developed on those sediments. Now preserved as peat, it is a mine of environmental information. From approximately 4000 to 1000BC the salt marsh grew outwards, towards (but not reaching) the entrance of the inlet. All that time the land was advancing, and the sea retreating, within the lagoon.

Then, around 1000BC came a critical turning point in the delicate balance between land and sea. The rate of rise in sea level overtook the rate of upward and outward growth of the salt marsh, and the sea began to advance, gradually eroding the edges and the surface of the peat and opening up salt-marsh creeks. In the first and second centuries AD, sea water was extracted from the upper reaches of these creeks to produce salt seasonally, in summer and early autumn. But the sea was continuing to advance and from the human point of view a crisis was reached around AD200. The surface of the peat became generally covered at high tide, the salt-workings were irrevocably flooded, and the salters retreated to the upland. This is the first recorded occasion when the inhabitants were driven back by the sea. The sea then sealed in the peat beneath silt and clay. In *c.*275, in the face of threatened Anglo-Saxon invasions, *Stutfall* fort was built on the hillside overlooking this marine inlet. After the fort had been abandoned in *c.*350, a landslip carried the south wall down into the marsh and the sea covered it with 3ft (1m) of silt. If the suggestion that this occurred in the sixth century is correct, the sea must have retreated very quickly after that, because written charters show that by 700 at least one large estate was already occupied and, probably more significantly, by 732 a sand dune had built out across the entrance to the inlet.

The massive shingle barrier had remained in a stable, middle-aged state providing protection from the sea for several thousand years. But this stability was coming to an end and the barrier began to break down. For a long time shingle had been accumulating at Dungeness, building out that point, with the result that the supply arriving from the south-west by means of longshore drift was trapped there, and none moved far north of Lydd. Consequently the barrier north of that was deprived of a fresh supply, and became increasingly thin. Eventually it was breached, and the tides flowed in, quickly 'capturing' the wide channel behind the barrier, and creating a wide inlet on which Romney was to be based. It is not yet possible to date this important breach, but a fishing village with an oratory, the forerunner of New Romney, was already established by 741. That port reached the height of its prosperity in the twelfth century, but declined when very serious silting affected the inlet in the thirteenth, in spite of far-reaching and no doubt very expensive efforts to prevent that happening.

By the early medieval period the barrier guarding the south side of the Marsh was also wearing thin. The reason was the same as that at New Romney — it was suffering from shingle starvation. The supply arriving from the south-west had diminished, and was insufficient to replace that being carried away towards Dungeness. The date at which the barrier was first breached there is very uncertain, but the scanty reports of *Old Winchelsea* in the second half of the eleventh century suggest that there was already some kind of sheltered haven. The salt works of Domesday also suggest that there was some kind of breach, which could have been open occasionally. Certainly by *c.*1200, when *Old Winchelsea* and Rye rose to prominence, there must have been a sheltered harbour. Since all the physical evidence was soon swept away, we shall never be certain about the surroundings of the old town and its port. A wide gap in the shingle barrier at an early date can be ruled out, since that would have allowed the sea to flood in over marshes which we have already seen were being reclaimed rather than lost in the twelfth and early thirteenth centuries. We can only guess that the town and the entrance to its harbour were probably protected by an outer spit, in some ways similar to that which developed east of the entrance to the so-called New Harbour of Rye in the eighteenth century (**75**). This kind of short-lived feature was characteristic of other historic harbours on the Sussex coast, such as Shoreham and Seaford. Whatever the circumstances, the storms of the thirteenth century tipped a finely-tuned balance, and over a period of some 50 years the sea swept away the barrier, and with it the town of *Old Winchelsea*.

When the barrier disintegrated, the sea flooded in across occupied marshland. That was the second occasion when we know the inhabitants had to retreat. But that time they were ultimately able to make a stand against the incursion. The *Great Wall*, a massive, remarkable feat of medieval engineering, crossed from one side of the Marsh to the other. The reasons for its success deserve some thought. It was a matter of time, space and resources. Even in the period of great storms, it took nearly 40 or possibly 50 years for the shingle barrier to break down, which put time on the side of the men who were constructing the wall. They had due warning. It presumably originated as a small structure, built progressively higher and wider as it became increasingly exposed to the sea. It was also significant that it stood several miles back from the barrier and the ground in front of it, even if only salt marsh would under normal conditions have broken the force of the waves long before they reached it. The storms of 1287-8, however, were far from normal. They must have generated surges that raised the sea to an unprecedented level and brought the waves right up to the wall. As for resources, financial responsibility was evidently determined by the *Laws and Customs* of the Marsh, and was divided between the landowners, most of whom were large ecclesiastical establishments, according to the acreage they held.

Although the topography shows that there were a number of breaches in the *Great Wall*, which may or may not have occurred in these specific storms, the accumulation of sediment on the outer side shows that by and large the wall withstood the onslaught of the sea. According to the Soil Survey up to 10ft (3m) was deposited outside the wall. Faced with a higher land level, the sea would not easily come so far inland again, and the pendulum swung in favour of general retreat by the sea. But although the 'new' land had become higher and in principle must have been some of the most attractive on the whole Marsh, it was not reoccupied quickly. Initially, the cost of repairing and maintaining the existing sea defences precluded expensive new reclamation schemes, and then after the Black Death in 1349 new land was no longer needed. The 'new' landscape of large fields shows that by the time re-reclamation did eventually proceed the economic scene had changed fundamentally, and extensive pastoral farming had succeeded the thirteenth-century mixed and arable system. This re-reclamation was underway by the beginning of the fifteenth century which, interestingly, suggests that the economy of the Marsh may have recovered from the fourteenth-century downturn sooner than that elsewhere.

The sea also began to replace the lost southern barrier. Shingle headlands began to

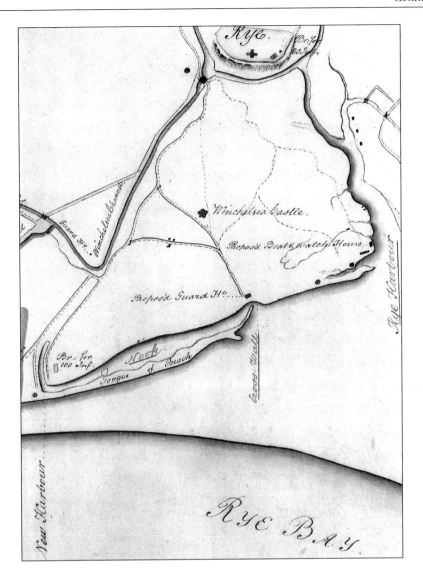

75 *The outer shingle spit named here as a 'Tongue of Beach' (shingle) which had developed outside*
the 'New Harbour of Rye' by 1807 is similar to spits which formed other historic harbours on the
Sussex coast, such as Shoreham and Seaford. Old Winchelsea *could have stood on an inner*
beach with a sheltered harbour similar to The Nook in front of it, perhaps connected to a channel
leading inland. It would have survived in calm weather, but great storms such as those of 1250
and 1252 would have broken through the outer spit, laying the town open to the full force of the
sea

grow from either side across the wide mouth of the inlet. On the east side of Rye Bay, waves under the influence of occasional south-east winds moved shingle spasmodically westwards, towards Rye. But ever since the thirteenth century the supply of shingle has been very limited, and the westward movement depleted the bank which had previously protected Broomhill. By about 1500 the shingle there had become an offshore bank that served to break the force of the waves in front of the maintained defence, the Kent Wall, which lay more than a mile (2km) to the north. Thus, in effect, a 'managed retreat' had been achieved. For the third time, the inhabitants were driven back by the sea. But on this occasion the retreat was much more localised than that in either *c*.200 or in the thirteenth century, because by then man had gained a considerable measure of control over environmental change. That coastline continued to migrate northwards, and in spite of entrepreneurial attempts to regain the lost land in Broomhill, no lasting innings was achieved there until *c*.1585.

Physical processes and human ingenuity were not the only factors which influenced the interplay between land and sea. Economic circumstances were also vital. As one historian wrote: 'when the economy is expanding, financial resources are available for the essential maintenance of sea banks, but when the economy is in decline, their maintenance is neglected. With a thriving economy, the sea is by no means sure to win'. The *Great Wall* is a striking example. It was built when the economy was booming, and it is quite doubtful whether it would have been erected if the economy had been weak at that time.

Ultimately, however, survival depended on the local inhabitants. From Saxon times onward the Marsh was owned mainly by the monasteries, none of which was on the Marsh. After the Dissolution of the Monasteries (1538-9), most of their land was transferred to lay landlords, but they too lived on the upland. The unsung heroes of survival, those who faced the daily slog of controlling the waters in order to preserve their lands and livelihood, were the tenants, sub-tenants and general workmen, some of whom were equipped with very special skills. Men such as Baldwin Scadeway and Doudeman took the initiative, no doubt employing a large labour force. Detailed records of routine and emergency administration have survived from more recent centuries. But we know almost nothing about the people who carried out the work. From rare documents such as the description of the Dymchurch Wall in *c*.1620 and the account book of work (literally) in the *Appledore Channel* we gain glimpses of what the work involved, by day and sometimes by night. In addition, the inhabitants faced the debilitating disease 'marsh ague', a form of malaria. The people of the Marsh certainly faced challenges that were not part of life on the upland. But in spite of that the Marsh survived, as a result of their constant vigilance.

Geography — like history — repeats itself. Each of the three tidal inlets provided an invaluable sheltered haven which became, for a limited time, a focus of human activity. Each of them eventually silted up, resulting in the loss of commercial activity for the local ports, and causing the townspeople to seek a new livelihood elsewhere. The evolution of the southern inlet has taken place recently, and is therefore relatively well understood through a mass of historic documents and a valuable range of historic maps, supplemented by the memories of people who remember developments in the last 60 years. The patterns of what occurred there can be used as models for what is likely to have happened elsewhere, at earlier dates. There is every reason to suppose that the problems that we know beset Rye must also have affected Romney. Simple processes like rapid silting when the tidal flow became reduced, the narrowing of channels, and clogging of the seaward side of sluices with silt, are all too familiar.

The special flat nature of the landscape gives it an unusual flexibility. For instance, the flow in the waterways is reversible. The *Wainway* is a good example of a large, natural, tidal channel which changed direction. In Saxon and Early Medieval time its mouth was at Romney, but once the sea had broken through the barrier near *Old Winchelsea*, it turned and entered the sea there, as shown several centuries later on the earliest maps. The artificial drainage was, and still is, arranged so that the water in the sewers can empty into the sea in two different directions: if one sluice is blocked, there is a good chance that the other will still be operational. The function of some walls, too, changed over time. For instance, the *Knelle Dam* was built across the west end of Wittersham Level, to keep the water of the Rother and the tides on the *west* side. But it is now used to keep floodwater in the 'wet level', on the *east* side.

This combination of geological, archaeological and historical research shows that some claims made by Dugdale and Elliott cannot now be substantiated, and must be dismissed. Neither the Dymchurch Wall nor the Rhee was of Roman origin. Indeed, since much of Romney Marsh proper was a tidal lagoon in Roman times, there was no need for it to be enclosed by sea walls! The available evidence shows that construction of the Dymchurch Wall was begun towards the end of the thirteenth century. And the Rhee cuts across late Roman creeks and early medieval field systems, and so must be later than those. It was an artificial watercourse dug to bring a supply of water across the Marsh to scour out the medieval port of Romney. The story that *Old Winchelsea* was washed away overnight is delightfully dramatic, but incorrect. Erosion began there in 1244 at the latest, and the effects of erosion were cumulative. The great storms of 1250 and 1252 greatly accelerated the process, but not until 1271 did a large part of the church of St Thomas fall. It is important to note that by 1280 *Old Winchelsea* was 'for the most part under the sea'. Edward I founded the new town on its hilltop, which was *before* the great storms of 1287-88, which are often credited with the destruction of the old town. Further detailed historical evidence indicates that the Rother changed its course from Romney to the southern inlet at the latest soon after 1250, rather than in 1287 as suggested by Camden.

This book is by no means the last word. Major questions remain unanswered. The record of storms contained in the Dungeness shingle needs to be explored, as do the changes in the barrier at inlets, particularly at Romney. The buried landscape of Romney Marsh proper should have much to tell us about the extent and nature of the Roman occupation, as should that of Walland Marsh about its use before 1287. The shrunken medieval town of New Romney cries out to be investigated (*see* **33**). Remarkably little is known about the enigmatic Rhee Wall, an outstanding work of medieval engineering. The archaeology of the river ports holds great promise, and a detailed history of the reclamations around Rye has yet to be written.

Research will continue. New teams will enter the field, new techniques will be developed, new information will be acquired, and with further time for reflection, new interpretations will be presented. The frontiers of knowledge are continually being pushed back. But the basic framework will not change, and it is hoped that the synthesis of results of recent research contained here will stimulate further interest and provide a basis on which others can build in future.

Glossary

Explanation of terms as they are used in this book

Artefact a man-made object, usually pottery or metalwork.

Blown up a sluice, or gutt, is described as being blown up when the entire structure of frame and gates is lifted bodily out of the ground by a high tide.

Briquetage very crude, very fragile fired clay or pottery associated with salt-making. It includes containers in which the brine was heated up; props to support those containers over the fires; and containers in which the salt could be transported. It is usually pale pink, though very occasionally black.

Coppice a dense wood in which the multiple trunks of the trees are cut down to their stumps every few years to provide a regular supply of poles and firewood. Very large quantities were produced in the Weald, brought down the rivers on lighters and exported through the ports of Rye and Winchelsea. Some coppices were regularly 'farmed' to produce the timber necessary for sea defences.

Crayers small vessels used for fishing and trading.

Delph ditch the ditch behind a bank, from which the soil for the bank was dug.

Enclosure *see Reclamation.*

Field-walking methodical collection of artefacts on ploughed fields. It involves establishing a grid pattern and collecting artefacts along the grid lines.

Fleet a former creek bed, which was enclosed from the sea before it silted up. The result is a long narrow strip below the water table, wholly or partially filled with rushes and other vegetation, a haven for wildlife.

Float	a dock, or place where vessels could float, a side-stream or backwater.
Gavelkind	a system of inheritance whereby a man's land was divided equally between all his sons or, where there were no sons, between his daughters. Also known as partible inheritance. This was peculiar to Kent but extended into the parts of Romney Marsh which are in Sussex.
Gravel	the commercial term for a mass of pebbles; *see shingle*.
Gutt	a wooden structure which controlled the outflow of water. An alternative name for a sluice which seems to have been applied only to the outflow of fresh water into the sea or a salt water inlet. However, as one innings built out from another, it often happened that eventually a gutt controlled the passage of water between one freshwater area and another.
Helmes	sand dunes.
Horizon	a specific layer of archaeological or geological material, or both.
Indraught	an area set aside for the storage of water, usually so that a large flow could be released at low tide in the hope of scouring silt out of the channel downstream. The source of the water was sometimes solely fresh water, but its effect was often amplified by taking in sea water at high tide.
Innings	*see Reclamation*. The verb 'to inn' means to reclaim.
Jetty	an early name for a groyne, a structure projecting into the sea. Its purpose was to arrest the longshore movement of shingle.
Kiddle fishing	shore fishing, whereby a net attached to a row of poles was strung down shallow beaches from the high water mark down into the sea to catch fish passing up the English Channel with the tide. The areas where this took place were known as kiddle grounds.
Lens	a discontinuous layer of geological or archaeological material.
Longshore drift	the process by which beach material is shifted laterally as a result of waves meeting the shore at an oblique angle.

Occupation layer	an area where human activity took place, though possibly only for a short time.
Porcupine	a metal device with numerous projecting spikes or teeth which was dragged down channels to stir up the sediments deposited in them.
Quay	a medieval term for a sea defence.
Reclamation	the conversion of wasteground into land which is then used either for arable or pasture on a year-round basis. It usually involved enclosing salt marsh which was accessible to the tides by constructing an earth bank round a certain area, organising pre-existing waterways and/or cutting new ones to convey the surface water of the new enclosure to an outlet through the bank. In this way an evolving, natural area became a managed, controlled unit which no longer evolved. The new areas of land were known variously as innings, enclosures or reclamations.
Resistivity	a geophysical technique that passes a small electrical current through the ground and measures the resistance to that current caused by buried features.
Reworked	archaeological or geological material that has been removed from its original position by the sea.
Scots	taxes exclusive to marshlands, levied to support the cost of maintaining either sea walls or the local main sewer and its outfall. They were paid in proportion to the acreage of each landholder, and were almost invariably paid by the tenants, otherwise known as *occupiers*, rather than by the *owners* of the land.
Sewer	an artificially controlled watercourse that conveys the surface water in a certain area of marshland towards the sea. The term was originally used on Romney Marsh, where it was adopted for the *Commissions of Sewers*, laws that were later applied to all the other marshlands in the country. It is important to note that the purpose of these watercourses was to remove fresh water: they were not intended to deal with domestic foul water.

Sherd   potsherds, broken pieces of pottery.

Shingle   a mass of water-worn, rounded-off pebbles. Over 99% of the Romney Marsh shingle is flint, non-crystalline silica, which has survived because it is harder than the other rocks found in south-east England. It occurs in a series of ridges, each of which was originally deposited as a beach thrown up by the sea. So every shingle ridge, although it may now be a considerable distance inland, was once the sea front. Shingle which is being commercially exploited is generally known as *gravel*.

Sluice   a structure of wood or masonry, with a gate or gates, that is used to regulate the flow of water in a sewer or river channel, where it flows out into the open sea or an inlet.

Spit   an elongated, often hooked strip of shingle projecting across an inlet, deposited by longshore drift.

Topography   all the elements in a landscape, which may be of natural or man-made origin.

Waterganges   a medieval term for watercourses.

Wet level   an area where river water is stored until it can be released through a sluice to the sea at low tide. This is necessary because rivers crossing marshland, such as the Rother, are tide-locked for part of the tidal cycle. About 600 acres (245ha) at the west end of the Wittersham Level are used as a wet level.

Further reading

Collard J. 1978 *Maritime History of Rye* (its value centres on the harbour in the last two centuries)

Colvin H.M. *et al.* (eds) 1982 *The History of the King's Works* iv (*see* 415-447 for Camber Castle)

Eddison J. and Green C. (eds) 1988 *Romney Marsh, Evolution, Occupation, Reclamation* Oxford Committee for Archaeology, Monograph 24

Eddison J. (ed) 1995 *Romney Marsh, The Debatable Ground* OUCA Monograph 41

Eddison, J., Gardiner M. and Long A. (eds) 1998 *Romney Marsh, Environmental Change and Human Occupation in a Coastal Lowland* OUCA Monograph 46

Edwards A. 1987 *The Romney Marsh story: a study in agricultural change* Farm Business Unit, Dept. of Agricultural Economics, Wye College

Green R.D. 1968 *Soils of Romney Marsh* Soil Survey of Gt Britain, Bull. 4

Johnson S. 1979 *The Roman Forts of the Saxon Shore* Paul Elek, London

Leslie K. and Short B. (eds) 1999 *An Historical Atlas of Sussex* (*see* 44-45 for recent work on New Winchelsea) Phillimore

Mayhew G. 1987 *Tudor Rye* Centre for Continuing Education, University of Sussex

Murray K.M.E. 1935 *Constitutional History of the Cinque Ports* Manchester

Murray K.M.E. 1945 *The Register of Daniel Rough, common clerk of Romney 1353-1380* (*see* the 68-page introduction) Kent Archaeological Society

Pratt M. 1999 *Winchelsea, a Port of Stranded Pride*

Teichman Derville M. 1936 *The Level and Liberty of Romney Marsh* Headley, Ashford

Vine P.A.L. 1972 *The Royal Military Canal* David & Charles

Winnifrith Sir John 1983 *History of Appledore* Phillimore

For other marshlands, and general landscape history:

Coles B. and J. 1986 *Sweet Track to Glastonbury: The Somerset Levels in Prehistory* Thames and Hudson

Darby H.C. 1940 *The Draining of the Fens* Cambridge

Darby H.C. 1940 *The Medieval Fenland* Cambridge, repr. 1974 David & Charles

Godwin, Sir Harry 1978 *Fenland: its Ancient Past and Uncertain Future* Cambridge

Hoskins W.G. 1967 *Fieldwork in Local History* Faber

Hoskins W.G. 1955 *The Making of the English Landscape* Hodder and Stoughton

Rackham O. 1986 *The History of the Countryside* Dent

Williams M. 1970 *The Draining of the Somerset Levels* Cambridge

Index

Names of lost places and names no longer in common use are printed in *italics*

All figure references are in **bold**